T0381213

MINDFUL RED FLAGS
AS YOU WALK
YOUR SPIRITUAL JOURNEY

How to Recognize Them and
Move Forward with Grace

DON DONINI
Foreword by John Shea

Balboa Press books may be ordered through booksellers or by contacting:

Balboa Press
A Division of Hay House
1663 Liberty Drive
Bloomington, IN 47403
www.balboapress.com
1 (877) 407-4847

Because of the dynamic nature of the Internet, any web addresses or links contained in this book may have changed since publication and may no longer be valid. The views expressed in this work are solely those of the author and do not necessarily reflect the views of the publisher, and the publisher hereby disclaims any responsibility for them.

This book is a work of non-fiction. Unless otherwise noted, the author and the publisher make no explicit guarantees as to the accuracy of the information contained in this book and in some cases, names of people and places have been altered to protect their privacy.

ISBN: 978-1-5043-9692-9 (sc)
ISBN: 978-1-5043-9693-6 (e)

Library of Congress Control Number: 2018901412

Print information available on the last page.

Balboa Press rev. date: 02/19/2018

BALBOA
PRESS
A DIVISION OF HAY HOUSE

I dedicate this book to Eileen Lucas, my spiritual mentor who started me on my spiritual journey.

Acknowledgements

My thanks to Joanna Gray, my editor and photographer extraordinaire, who has been by my side since second grade. To John "Jack" Shea for his wisdom and encouragement to make this book happen. To James Zullo, my life partner, for his unending love and support. To Mrs. Afton Wolfe, my high school English teacher who slowed me down enough to teach me to write. I also express my gratitude for R. Bruce Williams for his writing skills that he was willing to share with me. For Diane Shaughnessy for her marketing skills and support. For David Rueff, Emmy Bates, Carol Kats Willis, and Debbie Waldron Smith for always believing in me. For Anne Wolfe for holding me accountable to walking my journey. For the modern day mystics that I quote throughout my book. For you who are reading this right now. And foremost for the Christ, Spirit within, my personal God who breathes with me. I am forever grateful.

Foreword

The Right Fight
John Shea
Author and Theologian

Mindful Red Flags as You Walk Your Spiritual Journey: How to Recognize Them and Move Forward with Grace is a book that wants us to talk back.

This book does not fall into predictable categories. Although Don Donini shares and reflects on his experiences, this book is not a biography. Although he quotes a variety of spiritual teachers, this book is not survey of contemporary spiritual teachings. Although there is no shortage of opinion and advice, this is not an advice and opinion column expanded into book form. Donini is after something different.

He is the "guide by our side" and not "the sage on the stage." He is willing to point out some of the tentative and dangerous steps of spiritual journeys, but he does not want to take away our own stumbling advancements. At the end of each chapter, he gives us a prompt question for our own experiences and urges us to a website to continue the conversation he has started. He invites dialogue and explicitly values both our "yes" and our "no." Do we want to talk?

The theme is constant. As we connect more with our spiritual self and struggle to live out of that deeper consciousness, we are going to bump into and have to deal with the machinations of the mind. The thoughts and accompanying feelings of our minds are either collaborators or betrayers of our deeper spirit; and we are plunged into a process of inner observation and decision. Although social and cultural events are powerful and influential players in our comings and goings, how our minds process those events is the immediate subject matter of our spiritual development.

A Donini sampling of this subject matter is: being misunderstood, re-accessing work in the light of spiritual development, being and staying happy in a violent world, tithing as a paradoxical way of increase, persevering in meditation, driving affirmations into actions, resisting the temptation to substitute the spiritual for the medical, overcoming the fear to look into our darkness, realizing our much-vaunted knowledge can be used for good or bad, etc. If we don't have something to share and say on one of these topics, keep reading. One of the concerns of this book will certainly have our name on it. It is hard to escape these "red flags" without recognizing that at least one of them has been thrown onto the playing field of our own soul.

Many years ago, I was working with a community organization. At one meeting, the head organizer was checking on what everyone had done since the previous meeting. We all had specific tasks, and she wanted to know how they had gone. The first person to talk told a tale of woe. Everything he had tried had failed. The second to talk followed suit. As more talked, it became obvious that none of us had been able to do what we were supposed to do.

A different kind of silence came into the room, the silence that is the precursor of the question, "Why are we doing this since we are so bad at it?" The community organizer sensed this growing and despairing consciousness. She said, "Well, this has not been a good week, has it? We might be tempted to quit and say, 'Who needs this?' But we won't. We will go on because we are in the right fight."

I remembered this story as I read *Mindful Red Flags as You Walk Your Spiritual Journey: How to Recognize Them and Move Forward with Grace*. The spiritual life is often advertised as a solution to the problems and pains of physical, psychological, and social living. It is balm and blessing. But really it is specific type of struggle and persevering in it needs continual and intentional re-motivation. Don Donini's invitations to dialogue can help us, for they are surely part of the right fight.

Contents

Introduction

"The journey of a thousand miles begins with a single step." Lao Tzu

Are you "sick and tired of being sick and tired" and think you are ready to walk a spiritual path, or move to the second half of life as author Fr. Richard Rohr, OSF, talks about? Spirituality can mean different things to different people. Ultimately it is that part of us which is connected to something much bigger and greater than ourselves.

It is a hunger for a divine connection that goes far beyond satisfying than any physical hunger or need, especially in our fast-paced, modern digital age, as Agnus Gonxba, known to the world as Mother Teresa and Saint Teresa of Calcutta explains. She wrote:

"There is a spiritual poverty, that emptiness that you feel, that you are nothing— that is poverty of spirit. There is spiritual poverty knowing God, and not loving Him. In this Western world, there is much more of that than there is material poverty, which we face in Africa and in India, which is easy to satisfy. If there is a hungry woman, I give her a plate of rice—it is finished, I satisfied. But for people like that here, or in Rome or London or anywhere, a plate of rice is not going to satisfy. They don't need that. That terrible loneliness, that helplessness, that unwantedness, that complete darkness is very difficult [to satisfy]. It is great poverty."

Inspired by her wise words, I believe that what we need today is a personal, living relationship with God to enrich our spirituality – Spirit, Source, Inner Light, Truth, Universal Intelligence, Energy, or whatever is meaningful for you personally.[1]

---

[1] The writings of Mother Teresa of Calcutta © by the Mother Teresa Center, exclusive licensee throughout the world of the Missionaries of Charity for the works of Mother Teresa. Used with permission.

You may already have been walking a spiritual path for a short or even a very long time. Regardless of where you are on your journey, I am here if you would like to walk along with me through this book – and beyond – for new insights into your true self.

I love my spiritual life, so this book is not to be discounting but to be encouraging. I wrote it to provide helpful tools as we walk together on our spiritual journeys. There are human hurdles, however, to overcome as we choose to walk through life. I refer to these hurdles in the book as "red flags" that have the potential to set us back or throw us off course. But ironically by encountering these red flags, we know we are on the right path because they motivate us to overcome what has kept us stuck in the past and help us go further on our spiritual journey.

But what does being spiritual really mean? How do we get there? I once heard that religion is what we were born into and spirituality is something we choose. One could also say that authentic spirituality is invariably a matter of *"emptying the mind and filling the heart at the same time,"* as Richard Rohr wrote in an August 8, 2014, daily meditation based on his book, *Breathing Underwater: Spirituality and the Twelve Steps.*

"The spiritual path is never a straight line, but a back and forth journey that ever-deepens the conscious relationship of being chosen, of being a beloved, of Someone loving me more than I love myself, of Someone who is more me than I am myself." Richard Rohr

Walking the spiritual path is different for each one of us, but my personal story of spiritual transformation illustrates some of the typical challenges and obstacles – the "red flags" and "growing pains" – that come with spiritual growth.

After being laid off from my teaching position in 1989 after fourteen years, losing my apartment building where I lived, having to go bankrupt (does any of this sound familiar?), I was led to my spiritual mentor with whom I worked closely every week for two years. As it is said, when you need a teacher, a teacher will appear.

Ironically, these types of challenges when life seems the bleakest become our opportunities to grow if we choose to look at them as growing pains. The first line in Dr. Scott Peck's book, *The Road Less Traveled*, states "Life is difficult." I learned he is saying that if we realize this, that life is difficult and choose not to run away from it, face our difficulties, and challenges head on (seeing them as opportunities) it can teach us glorious things on the way to attaining bliss in our lives. I know what you may be thinking: Don Donini, I don't need another opportunity. I get it, as I furiously told a therapist who had offered me that advice. I know you

would never believe I needed therapy, right? But I found this to be true as I began to walk my path, and still find it true as I continue my spiritual journey.

I also hear people say, well when I get there I will be happier, be blissful, find life easier. Sorry, but there is no place to "get to." If you think that the path ends and that there is a final stop, it doesn't. The spiritual journey is a lifelong *process* and not a destination. As Helen Keller once said, "Life is a succession of lessons which must be lived to be understood. It is an ongoing venture and adventure to change and grow."

Please note, however, that it does get easier because we acquire more tools as we walk along our paths. Becoming aware of the red flags I talk about in this book will add more tools to help you over the rough spots. Of course, we must take action and use those tools to get the benefits. They do no good just sitting in our tool boxes.

So what can you expect from this book? First, I emphatically teach that we must be open, ready and willing to have a better life. I suggest that you be open when reading this book – take what you want and leave the rest behind. When you start to judge this material, I suggest that you take a belly breath and discern what is your Truth, what is yours to learn before judging, what fits for you now as you walk your path. Discern through contemplation and meditation.

What is a belly breath?

"Inhale for a count of four, hold for a count of seven, and exhale for a count of eight. You can just do it once and get a nice effect, although I usually like to do it. Repeat the cycle as many times as you like. For the last 20 years this breathing pattern has helped me through panic attacks, bumpy airplane rides, Los Angeles traffic, audition jitters and insomnia. It is a miracle worker. Inspiration shares the same root word with and respiration, and it is no accident that a deep breath can both relax us and bring us closer to God." Sam Bennett, Daily Word, July/August 2017, Unity Publications

Also, please note that I have chosen my words very carefully in the book, so as you read, please ponder on words I use. Some words speak to us differently than for others. Words become personal depending on where we are in our experiences. You will find my teachings very practical. In college I always loved watching, *Gunsmoke* on TV, and my roommate would tease me and say that the reason I liked it is because the writers of this show had written it for a seventh grade mentality. I instead call it practical. And it is ok if you are too young to remember *Gunsmoke*. If so, bless your youthful hearts too.

As I tell stories, I do realize that it is only my side of the story. I cannot be in your heads. "We are the only thinkers in our mind," as metaphysician Louise Hay writes. When I speak about negatives like hurt and betrayal, these are coming from our humanness. We need to acknowledge these human experiences that go on in our lives but also remember that we are perfect in spirit.

I was also inspired to write this book for the Millennials and future generations to come to give them guidance for their own spiritual journeys in the second half of life. I am concerned that it may be even more challenging for them to find their true, spiritual selves than for us today because of the constant "noise" of cell phones, texts, email, social media, podcasts that permeate the brain 24/7. As technology increases, the noise increases. But as I have mentioned before, we have to shut out the noise, turn it off, and be still to discover our true path and grow spiritually. It was challenging enough in my generation to turn off the stereo or the radio, or turn the ringers off on our landline phones (I sound a million years old here!). Today, many people have headphones or earbuds attached to their heads constantly as if these devices are a part of their physical body. But just like the silver lining in the cloud, today there is also motivational and relaxing music and sounds to listen to through these electronic devices that may help people connect with themselves spiritually. One of the goals of my book is to get people to that happy medium of living spiritually in a noisy, high-tech world.

The author D. H. Lawrence said, "The world fears a new experience more than it fears anything. Because a new experience displaces so many old experiences." Lawrence also said, "A true *inner experience* changes us, and human beings do not like to change." I invite you now to put aside your fears of new experiences and change. Get started or continue on your spiritual path with me. Let's journey together past the red-flag obstacles to get ever closer to our Truth.

I would love to know what you are thinking as you read each chapter, so please share with me your thoughts, concerns, and joys on my website at www.dondoninibook.com. This website is not a personal mentoring service, but rather a way to provide feedback and continue the discussion of spiritual red flags among readers of this book. If you are interested in the spiritual mentoring services that I provide via Skype video conferencing, please click the "Contact Me" link on my website.

Saying Yes When You Want to Say No

"If you cannot say no, how can I trust your yes?" – Dr. James Zullo, Ph.D.

At our first meeting my spiritual mentor recommended a book entitled, "Why Do I Say Yes When I Want to Say No?" (now out of print, but check Amazon.com in the out of print books section). She was suggesting that I would have no time to grow spiritually because I could not say no to taking on so many other commitments besides my full time job and two part time teaching jobs.

Saying yes seemed to be embedded in my DNA. I remember my dad never saying no, especially to the nuns and priest in our parish who relied on Dad to repair things at the convent and rectory. He volunteered for just about everything whenever they asked and even when they didn't ask. Did he think that would earn his way to heaven more easily by always saying yes? His tendency to never say no to others did not create a peaceful relationship with my mom. He had no time for her and his children. So saying yes all of the time was what I learned as an obligation and "the right thing to do" as I grew up.

Author Vernon Howard, known for his life-healing books, talks about the "yes-traps" that can snare us into saying yes when we really want to say no. His 10 traps mentioned in his book *The Power to Say No* are spiritual red flags to watch out for:

1. *You feel you might seem unfriendly.*
2. *It relieves nervous indecision.*
3. *You fear a domineering person.*
4. *It avoids your anxious explanations.*
5. *You have always said yes.*
6. *Someone has promised you a reward.*
7. *It makes you seem kindly.*

8. *You want to be accepted.*
9. *Everyone else is saying yes.*
10. *You want to avoid unpleasant reactions.*

You've probably heard the expression, "What part of no do you not understand?" How many times have we heard that we can't be everything to everybody? And here's the kicker: Being everything to everyone doesn't guarantee more love in our lives. Are people going to love us more or will we be happier if we always say yes to their needs and demands? Not really. People pleasing, in fact, can bring about more stress in our lives rather than happiness, and may even be the underlying cause of chronic overweight and eating disorders. As Tricia Nelson, the author of "Heal Your Hunger: 7 Simple Steps to End Emotional Eating" cautions: "One of the most common traits among emotional eaters is people pleasing. Those who struggle chronically with food and weight are typically caught in a trap of taking on too many projects and doing too many favors in an effort to please others."

By saying no to take care of ourselves we can teach others to do the same, and as a result, show them the way to grow spiritually, also. Most importantly, if we want to keep growing spiritually ourselves, learning to say no and sticking to it is a necessity. If always saying yes, there will be little time to develop and live from Spirit. Yes, I will chair your committee. Yes, I will help you move. Yes, I will coach the team. Yes, I will plan the church event and host it. Yes, I will be on the condo board. Yes, I will always drive the children, and yes, I will do everything for my aging parents (even when other siblings are around). Yes, I will go out dancing, to the movie, for coffee, for dinner tonight (even though I would rather stay home because I am exhausted). Yes, yes, sure I will be the boy scout or girl scout leader. Yes, I will decorate your party. I will, I will, I will until there is no energy left for my own life needs, let alone a spiritual journey. If this sounds like the "yes" litany you have been saying, it's time to stop, sit quietly, and meditate on why you can't, or don't want to, say no.

You will probably realize that there are many perceived payoffs for always saying yes when you really want to say no. Maybe we do it so people will like us or love us, or to feel needed, or to not disappoint important people in our lives such as our family or pastor. Sometimes we say yes out of peer pressure to fit in with the group and "step up" to serve. Maybe we want to stay busy and avoid dealing with our difficult life issues, or maybe we're afraid of how we will change as we grow spiritually. For myself, I said yes to avoid confrontation, something I struggle with to this day. The truth is that there is no guarantee that any of this will be to your advantage as you constantly say yes. I am all about being service-oriented, but not when it is detrimental to my spiritual growth.

So what is the way around this red flag? Start giving yourself permission to say no when you don't want to say yes. To anyone. To anything that you do not have the time, energy, or desire to do. When you start saying no is when your spiritual journey will get back on track. But it won't be easy at first. If you have been a "yes person" and you start taking care of yourself by saying no, it will take several, persistent "no's" to the people who are used to you saying yes before they realize you have grown to the point that you're now making a conscious choice between yes and no.

Also, know that you do not have to answer immediately when someone asks you to do something. Take a deep breath and then tell the person that you need time to think about it, check your calendar, check with your partner – but most of all to give yourself time to sit quietly and discern whether or not you really want to do – or have the time and energy – what you're being asked to do.

To say no, I give you permission to use "What part of no do you not understand?" Practice saying, "No, I have to take care of myself. I have to get things off my plate. I'm just not available." Or just say no. "No is a complete sentence," as author Anne Lamott reminds us, and your "no" requires no further explanation. Really. I believe in you that you have the courage and persistence and know how to say no. Blessings on your journey.

Affirmation: *My "no" means no, and my "yes" means yes. I discern through Spirit what is right for me before I answer yes or no.*

Have you had to learn to say no to start and progress on your spiritual path? How did that feel? Has it become easier to say no? Please share on my website, www.dondoninibook.com.

Misunderstood Again

"I'm just a soul whose intentions are good. Oh Lord, please don't let me be misunderstood."
"Don't Let Me Be Misunderstood" – Song recorded by Eric Burdon and the Animals

I was so excited about my new-found spiritual self that I asked to do a New Thought Unity eulogy for a distant relative who took his life. It would have been appropriate if it hadn't been a funeral mass in a Catholic church in front of my conservative Catholic family. Yes, and they also thought that I lost my mind. I realize now that I was setting myself up to be misunderstood.

When we get a taste of living spiritually we can be misunderstood. As we are directed by Spirit, we may appear aloof, selfish, or non-caring. We may not be any of these things, but we appear that way especially to people who have just started a spiritual path, or people who are steeped in religiosity and have yet to choose a personal God. People who choose not to help themselves when help is right in front of them. Those who are in denial and remain victims. God does love it all. Some people want spirituality without doing the work, and they misunderstand us to the point that they lash out at us. I remember something that happened when I was spiritual director of a New Thought Church. During the hospitality hour after a service, one of the congregants lashed out and yelled at me in front of the group. My *humanness* felt disrespected. Also, I have found that rookies just starting on their path become "large and in charge" (not physically, but self-righteously). They are chosen to be on the church board, and the result is usually not pretty. I have seen these know-it-alls sway the groups to the point of extinction.

When you become more spiritually aware, people may think that you are being impatient, mean or short with them when you are just being more assertive and taking care of yourself. People may think that we are opportunists when we are actually just being realists. Your motives and responses in different situations may often be misunderstood, especially by people who have not grown spiritually as much as you have, or at all. It's a red flag to assume that everyone you know or meet has grown as much as you have or in the same way – even if your intentions are good.

We may also choose to be impatient with those of unlike mind, or with those who stay stuck in negativity or stay in their religion of birth. Our impatience can be interpreted as being mean or aloof, but it becomes a red flag for us when our impatience becomes abusive or hurtful to others, or even to ourselves and we grow and learn more along our spiritual path. As Louis Hay writes, "Impatience is resistance to learning."

I remember attending a 12 Step meeting for the first time, and being a rookie I thought that the person running the meeting didn't like me when she was just being assertive and was working her program. I wasn't as far along in my growth as she was, so I misunderstood her approach. But later I began to understand. As I grew on my own path, I felt that everyone had grown like me. Freer like me. Happier like me. More peaceful like me, even in the face of painful moments in my life. I felt rejection at times when I had chosen to just grow in a different way than others. Some people would ask why I was choosing this spiritual path when they liked me more before the way I used to be. They didn't understand that a spiritual path is something that we don't choose, but something we are led to.

Our families may misunderstand us the most sometimes. When I was first working through my own personal struggles as I began my spiritual path, I felt misunderstood by my parents. They did not understand why I needed a new spiritual path and mentor when I was already raised Catholic. My spiritual mentor advised me to put some distance between me and parents, and anyone who was authoritarian or controlling in my life, for a time. Then my parents came to visit me and drove the 6 hours to my home. It was a Sunday and I ran out to the driveway to meet them because I was so excited to see them. The first thing out of my mother's mouth was, "Did you go to Mass today?" And then my dad said, "Are you still seeing that quack?", referring to my spiritual mentor. You see, now I was different than these more conservative Catholics that I grew up with. But didn't I feel that different. After all, I had been taught – indoctrinated – that the Catholic Church was the only true church established by God, and if I professed my faith at any other church but a Catholic church I would go to hell. Well, I was not there anymore. (However, I am grateful for discovering God early in life through my Catholic education.) I did not address the Mass issue with my mom, but responded to my dad. I said, "It is either seeing my mentor or becoming alcoholic (which runs in the family), or commit suicide. Which would you choose?" My parents never mentioned either issue again.

I also began to see and hear things in my family for what they really were – such as criticism or anger hidden beneath a cloak of humor or teasing. One Christmas I was visiting my brother and his family. He was always a jokester, but this time his joke didn't sit well with me. It no longer felt good. As my niece and nephew were opening their gifts from me, my brother laughed and said, "Oh, it is another love book from Uncle Don." I had become concerned about my niece and nephew's future as they were growing up in our addictive family dynamics, so I would give them a tried and true self-help book for their libraries each year to refer to throughout their lives. But my brother didn't understand that I was indeed showing love to his children with my gifts, so he showed his misunderstanding – or criticism? – through his joke.

My brother probably thought that his joking was showing me love in our family's dysfunctional way, but this time it felt hurtful to me. I again felt misunderstood because I had grown beyond that dysfunctionality. I had begun to live more healthy and peacefully. So, if you are a serial jokester please, note that there is a lot of truth in jest. Your joking can be very insensitive and hurtful for people. So another red flag here is to not acknowledge that there is a lot of truth in jest. I was tactless in my joking a lot of the time before starting on my spiritual journey, and as a result I lost friends because I was not conscious that my joking was hurting them.

I was also misunderstood by a dear friend. She was getting re-married, and she asked me to decorate her home for their wedding reception with floral arrangements. I delivered the flowers and went to the wedding ceremony. My family was there and my extended family of the bride from my hometown. I chose to not attend the reception back at the house, because I knew I would experience the same energy that I grew up with – and that would be too painful for me since I had become more divinely self-aware. I was no longer letting them play the guilt card as they insisted that I come to the reception. It was not easy to say no. I told them that I did not feel well (I was emotionally worn out) and had to go home, which I did. The bride called when I got home and left a voice mail cursing at me for not being there. I know that she meant well and missed me attending, but I just could not do it. My spirit would not let me.

So whether they are family members, friends, or co-workers, people who are stuck in the first half of life and living out their own drama and that of others may expect us to live in their freneticism. When we refuse to do so and instead live more peacefully around them, it makes for misunderstanding. It makes us look as if we aren't caring about them when really we are just not buying into their drama any more. (But remember that even drama queens are loved by God unconditionally!) As Erma Bombeck once wrote, "The truth will set you free but first of all it will piss people off." Our goal is that other people will notice how we now handle our life situations more peacefully and quietly, and ask us how we got to that place. This is when we can share our growth and help them start or better continue on their spiritual journey.

Affirmation: *I speak my truth with love.*

Have there been times when you felt misunderstood on your spiritual journey? Tell me your story. Please share on my website, www.dondoninibook.com.

Don't Quit Your Day Job. At Least Not Yet.

"Tell me, what is it you plan to do with your one wild and precious life?" – Mary Oliver

For many of us as we walk our spiritual paths, our jobs, relationships, and other life situations may start to no longer serve us or feel "right." You could say that we have outgrown them. Work becomes unfulfilling. Marriages go stale. The thrill has gone out of the activities or causes that used to bring us joy. Yes, we change as we grow spiritually, and it's nothing to feel guilty or ashamed about. It's all a natural part of your spiritual transformation. But it's not a license to act impulsively. And making impulsive decisions is a major red flag that can throw you way off course on your path.

Yet, sometimes the urge to run away is just overwhelming. As we let go of our false self and let our true self come to light, integrity becomes emphatic in our lives, as well as humility. For example, on the job we choose to no longer step on people to climb the corporate ladder. Then when see those power hungry co-workers, managers, and employers who are walking all over people to get to the top without being in integrity, it becomes more difficult to stay on the job. There is nothing wrong with people wanting to advance in their career dreams, goals and desires if it is done with integrity and without demeaning people. Or sometimes the company's vision or mission is now out of sync with our newfound integrity. When we feel and see this we want to jump ship and quit. The energy there is so very hard to take any longer. But please don't quit. Wait. Gather information from reliable and trusted sources, discern, and listen to Divine guidance before handing in that two-week notice.

Discernment is getting all your opinions and information and then sitting quietly (cell phones and computers off, please) and asking the Universe, God, Source – Divine Mind, Infinite Consciousness,

Before we make an important decision, we should ask questions and weigh the pros and cons of each options – examining the value, necessity, and the long-term implications. Once we have the information we need, we use spiritual discernment to invite the wisdom of higher mind and listen within." Unity Minister and Professor Claudell County, Daily Word.

Yahweh, Spirit, Allah or however you define Divine guidance – whatever you call Divine guidance) what to do. Share your desires with the Divine on what you see yourself doing, also, and then *listen*. Did I say *listen*? Yes, listening is an important step in the process.

Oh, and trust that guidance will be given in God's time. As someone I know advanced on her spiritual journey, she was guided to do tarot card readings and wanted to make a living doing it. So instead of quitting her full time job right away as a licensed social worker in a hospital, she was permitted to work part-time where she grew her tarot card business. Eventually she was able to quit the hospital job when she could support herself doing what she loved to do – the tarot card readings. Discern and be guided. Then affirm your decision. You may have to lower your lifestyle to have the work and the life that makes your heart sing, but affirm that, "I have that ideal job where I am highly compensated financially for my skills."

There are many people who want a career or job that harmonizes with their new self-awareness. I get it and I am the first to ask someone how they would segue out of an outgrown job or marriage, especially after I hear how they have been miserable for years. I hear them when they say "this job just isn't right for me anymore" or "he/she isn't the person I married." That's not surprising, because we change and grow and take risks every day – and that is the only way we can grow spiritually.

But we need not act out of haste or impulsiveness without weighing the consequences. Financial experts advise having 6 months to two years of salary saved up, and taking the time to build your brand and clientele before transitioning into a new career. I was advised to do that when I transitioned from owning my own business to a career in body work, massage therapy and reiki. I was burned out as a business owner, but who knows? You may find that your current corporate job starts to make your heart sing as you continue to grow spiritually.

I was talking to someone still working in the corporate world after much self-awareness work. Her spiritual growth was initiated after surviving breast cancer. It's what I call her conversion experience entering the second half of life. If you've ever worked in a corporate environment, you know that the job description never calls for you to "work more from spirit" so it's not surprising that you may feel a disconnect from who you are now and the corporate culture you spend most of your time in.

"I no longer fit the mold: The corporate speak no longer resonates, the opportunities here don't look so enticing," she told me. "But I am here 10 hours a day. So as difficult as the disconnect feels at times, I am using my job today as a further opportunity for more self-growth. I'm practicing things I've learned, including setting healthy boundaries. You're not going to find me huddled in my cube working at 11:00 p.m. after everyone else around me has been home for hours. I'm leaving by 5:30 p.m. because the work will still be there tomorrow. I, of course, want to find a new job that aligns better with who I am now. But I can't just quit my job. I'm choosing to be responsible in supporting myself with the lifestyle I am accustomed to having until I know where I am going."

So, again, I urge you to wait. Do not quit that job until you have sat quietly to discern and dream about the career that will replace what you have at the present. Be still and listen to Divine guidance so that you can joyfully answer the poet Mary Oliver's question, *"Tell me, what is it you plan to do with your one wild and precious life?"*

Affirmation: *I have an ideal job where I am highly compensated financially for my skills.*

After embracing your true spiritual self are you planning to leave, or did you leave, the corporate world rather abruptly? How did it play out for you? Please share on my website, www.dondoninibook.com.

Happiness is Our Light

"Ever since happiness heard your name, it has been running through the streets trying to find you." – Hafez

Has happiness found you yet? Are you happy? What does happiness mean to you? I call happiness our "light." It is Divine light that we develop as we walk our spiritual path. It is that place within us that makes us say, "Thank you, God! Thank you, Spirit!" with joy every morning and take off on life adventures with our loved ones or on our own. It is that light that radiates an inner peace and joy that attracts good people, situations, and things into our lives. As the Persian poet Hafez wrote centuries ago, happiness is trying to find you right now! But we are so busy chasing the buck and trying to keep up with the Joneses. We are so busy "doing" that we do not know how to "be". Between the stress of daily life and staring at our phones and tablets, it seems there is little time to embrace happiness. I am not saying that today's electronics are not good, but only that we need to use them in ways that support our happiness, not deter us from it.

Most of all, beware of some really dark places along the way that threaten to block your light – your happiness – because there is so much fear and negativity in the world today. Every time we log onto the Internet, watch television or listen to talk radio the media promotes fear through sensationalism and what some call propaganda. It's like the Eagles song, "Dirty Laundry" – it seems that we love hearing about the "dirty laundry" of conflicts and drama. And in the Internet age these negative messages can bombard us constantly if we let them. Think about some people who wear an Apple iWatch that delivers these news blasts *immediately*. And the sad part is that many of us buy into the negativity – a huge red flag that our light of happiness is being blocked.

Even people who are a part of the media and entertainment world are starting to take notice. In an interview in the April 2017 edition of *American Way* magazine, actor Charlie Hunnam expresses his aversion to social media groups like Facebook and Instagram as a roadblock to happiness. This resonates for me because I was once taught that unhappiness is the result of comparing ourselves to others' looks, fortune, relationships, etc.

"I am so baffled by the whole phenomenon of social media," Hunnam said. "To me, it speaks to going the wrong direction, trying to fill up this gaping hole that we all have in us. I am not interested in what anyone had for breakfast or what they think of these shoes they're wearing or where they're on vacation. This instant ability to like, dislike and cast immediate snap judgements on things and being encouraged to do so proliferates into our everyday existence. I think it's incredibly corruptive of our ability to just live without judgment, which is clearly the path to happiness."

Sadly, the happiness of our younger generation is at risk, as well, as they rely on social media as substitutes for real-life, face-to-face interactions with other people. In "Have Smartphones Destroyed a Generation?", an August 2, 2017 article in *The Atlantic* magazine, Jean M. Twenge explores the lifestyle of what she calls the "iGen" or a generation of young people raised on the Internet and social media who seek happiness in their Smartphones, tablets, and other electronic devices – all at the risk to their mental health and personal social interactions. As Twenge writes, "Rates of teen depression and suicide have skyrocketed since 2011. It's not an exaggeration to describe iGen as being on the brink of the worst mental-health crisis in decades. Much of this deterioration can be traced to their phones."

The 2016 U.S. presidential campaign was yet another prime example of the threat to happiness in our lives. The candidate who was elected president promotes violence, calls people names to deface and shame them as he puts down their cultural beliefs, their skin color, their sexual identity, and even their body shape. He degrades women – even his own daughter – by making crude sexual remarks that he passes off as "locker room talk." Yet, he was elected and continues to bring drama and conflict to the world, which is promoted heavily by the media and leads to more unhappiness to people everywhere. Sad. But we can avoid the red flag of believing in this drama and instead choose happiness as we walk our spiritual path of positive action and unconditional love.

Another example hits closer to home for me. By buying into the fear of recent terrorism in the world last Christmastime, one of my soul mates chose not to come to Chicago to visit and celebrate with us. The media blast about terrorist attacks got to her big time. She was afraid to travel on the train or to be in Union Station in fear of terrorist bombs. She was afraid to go to the theater where we had tickets to a joyful musical, because terrorists had targeted a theater in Paris. Because she bought into the fear from the internet and the media, she was unable to come share in our fearless happiness and joy. And she has a lot of joy to share. Her fear was real and it paralyzed her for a time. Sad and heartbreaking.

I am not saying that there are not negative or fearful situations out there, but we need to discern carefully what we choose to buy into. I'm also not saying that we won't sometimes feel "blue" or experience sadness, grief, and pain. Don't deny these feelings. In fact, sadness is said to be an avenue to happiness because we can put a light around our emotions and let them go. Earlier in my own spiritual walk my goal was to feel happy over 50% of the time. It's easier said than done, but very workable and possible to achieve.

> *"We have to be more than positive in our lives! We must cultivate the courage to look within our own hearts to feel, see, and transform the darkness into Light." Reverend Patty Pipia, www.revpatty.com*

Happiness is our birthright, but somehow it is rewarding to stay on our pity pots. We sometime want to stay addicted to pain, unhappiness. I always get a kick out of asking someone how the day is going and they reply, "Ok, so far". So far? That predisposes the happy part of the day. It is like we are programmed to wait for the other shoe to drop. Also, it's a red flag if you start buying into the unhappiness of people and things, situations around you just to be liked and accepted. And to feel that everyone's light is as bright as yours. Some people may even be scared of your light, not knowing what to do with it because your happiness confuses them. People will either run away from your light or run toward it and embrace it.

The good news is that as we grow on our spiritual paths we become happier. As we affirm positively, we think more positive thoughts. Sitting quiet with ourselves every day, we find that being happy becomes a habit. Feeling free goes along with being happy. People will say to me, "Why are you smiling?" Because I am a happy person. Again, don't be surprised if being happy confuses people, especially those folks that are unhappy, not spiritually aware or self-aware. Also, as we grow spiritually, we become rather fearless a lot of the time, not in a dangerous sense, so it can be difficult to be with and especially live with someone who lives a fearful existence. Stay "prayed up" if this is the case.

As I became more self-aware by walking my spiritual journey, I remember going out for dinner and sitting there reading a book and I was just radiating happiness. When delivering my food to my table my server said," What are you on? Whatever it is I want some." I told her God and loving myself. She wasn't expecting that. When we would go to my small hometown to visit my elderly father who was a widower, his girlfriend would often say, "Donald, you bring joy when you come down!" It was Divine connection that I had worked on while walking my path, but I did not elaborate that to her.

So the lesson here is to stay "prayed up" to remain happy and be able to shine your light in the midst of fearful, unhappy people and world situations. And some of the time it will even wear off on those negative souls who have not yet found their light. Be still and let happiness find you.

Affirmation: *I am lighthearted and happy.*

How do you remain happy in this chaotic, unsettled world? Can you measure how much your happiness has increased since you began walking your spiritual path? Please share on my website, www.dondoninibook.com.

Don't Be Afraid to Give

"Money is like love: the more you give away, the more you have." – Edwene Gaines

When I first heard the word "tithe" – an often used term for "free will giving" – it left a bad taste in my mouth, so to speak, because it conjured up the old messages from my religion of birth – mainly the old fear that there is never ever enough. Some people also think that religious and spiritual teachings should somehow be free or worth little. If you believe either of these negative thoughts about tithing, it is a red flag that will be detrimental to your spiritual growth. If the word "tithing" bothers you or brings up negativity, substitute the word "giving" or whatever term resonates with you.

It took me a long time to tithe even after I grew spiritually. I thought I could not afford to tithe, and then I found out that I could not afford *not* to tithe if I wanted good and money to keep flowing in my life. Some people still resist tithing and wonder why the circulation of the their good seems to have dried up. We know that if we want more of anything we have to give more of what we want. Not tithing also can also keep us in lack consciousness and reinforce the negative thought that there will never be enough. In her book *The Dynamic Law of Prosperity*, Catherine Ponder puts this concept in clear perspective: "Tithing is an ancient law of prosperity. It is a protection from negative experiences. Tithing brings definite financial increase. Tithing brings harmonious progress in relationships. Tithing brings peace of mind. It is the best investment you can make in peace, health and plenty."

Yet another red flag here is to stop tithing after more prosperity has begun to flow into your life. You may think you have all that you need now, and therefore have no need to tithe anymore. But that is not how the spiritual law of tithing works. As Edwene Gaines, author of *The Four Spiritual Laws of Prosperity: A Simple Guide to Unlimited Abundance*, writes, "The more you give away, the more you have." Stopping your tithe stops the flow of prosperity – and stunts your spiritual growth.

Personally, I have found that I cannot continue to grow in my Truth without tithing. When I started tithing it was very painful for me. I was stuck in thinking that there was not enough and would never be enough. Initially, I gave begrudgingly, which is not unusual when some people start to give. Now I willingly, lovingly tithe each time I get paid. Giving to God first is universal law. Don't worry so much about the percent of your tithe. Just start and continue to give regularly. You can always increase it as you grow spiritually and financially. It really doesn't matter what your income is, as long as you give something. Understand that when we give we do not lose, but gain. Yes, loss is inevitable in life, but I haven't experienced it from actively embracing generous giving. Today, I want for nothing, and I find that I always have enough.

The experience of one of my fellow spiritual seekers powerfully illustrates the mystery of tithing. My friend was directing a performance of a Broadway musical at a university, but he soon saw that he might have to cancel the show because he did not have enough male actors for the show. He had eight, but needed at least 12. Although he was doing his prayer work and affirming a positive outcome, he still did not have the complete cast he needed. Then he reconsidered his tithing practice, and wrote a large check to tithe to a New Thought church he was attending. The next day, he had 16 male actors for the show – more than enough to continue with the production. My friend attributed his success to his willingness to tithe generously, even though he was at risk of having to cancel his show.

So I see you letting go of any fear around starting or continuing to tithe. Get ready for even more glorious things are appearing in your life.

Affirmation: *I willingly and lovingly tithe to God first.*

What do you think? Have you seen your monies, relationships, time, and talents multiplied from tithing . . . or not? Do you have a tithing story? Please share on my website at www.dondoninibook.com.

Meditation is as Important as Breathing

"Peace comes from within. Do not seek it without." – Buddha

Meditation is where all answers are, all peace is, all healing is, all blessings are. It is Divine guidance. Meditation is to your spiritual life as what breathing is to your physical body. The practice is essential to being vibrantly alive.

Hay House Publishing CEO Reid Tracy gives us a personal example of that vibrancy: *"I practiced clearing my mind and I soon became hooked because I felt much better almost every time I found/made the time to do my meditation. I felt more energy after I meditated as well as more calm and peaceful, especially during stressful situations at work and home with my family. It seems simple but the results are literally life-changing. And it's just from making 10 minutes a day to clear your mind."*

Meditation or contemplative prayer plays a major role in our spiritual growth. So the red flag here is not considering meditation essential to living and not taking the time to meditate. We may make excuses for not meditating, such as how can I fit this in my day, not enough time, etc. Not that these excuses are not valid in our everyday lives. Meditation is said to bring peace and serenity into our soul and help heal our emotional pain. You may have to get up 15-30 minutes earlier to meditate – you are worth it. Get a cup of coffee and set it next to you as you become quiet. I initially had to set a timer to sit still. I just started at five minutes, so be patient with yourself if being still seems difficult at first. There are even timer apps for your cell phone, such as Insight Timer and Asana Rebel, that you can use anywhere, any time. No matter what technique you choose to help you sit quietly, the practice of repeating a word, mantra, or simply conscious breathing will also help.

Believe it or not, you can go to your quiet place even amidst the chaos of the workplace. If your job starts to overwhelm you, or if a project is slowing down, find a quiet place to be alone. Just go into the restroom and sit in a stall and take three or four belly breaths. Just sit quietly for five minutes focusing on your breath, not on the tasks at hand, knowing that you will be guided. You'll be surprised how things will fall into place. Or if you have just a moment or two, just stop and picture in your mind a "feel good" place like a beautiful garden or a lovely beach. Breathe in the vibrant colors and glorious scents. Then breathe out, releasing any stressful thoughts. Afterwards, your work will feel different because you are approaching it with Divine guidance.

Another red flag here would be following the opinions of others instead of Divine guidance.

We are bombarded with opinions from family and friends, and from our own "monkey chatter minds" as we share our joys and struggles. Processing all of these opinions in our mind are crazy making. This is why meditation is so very important. We take all the opinions and sit quietly and ask God to speak to us around all of these joys and /or struggles, and all of these opinions. In meditation we go to that Christ Center, our heart center, the chakra for *our* Divine guidance to answer our concerns, trusting yourself to make responsible choices. Not my will but thy will be done. I know what I want but what does Spirit, God want for me?

Richard Rohr points us toward meditation and contemplation as the way to hear God's answer: *"Contemplative prayer is a practice of kenosis or self-emptying. At its most basic, contemplation is letting go of our habitual thoughts, preferences, judgments, and feelings. Although life itself—love, awe, or suffering—is often the catalyst for our transformation, contemplation is a daily, small death to false self and ego. It prepares a spacious place in which resurrection of True Self can occur."* (Daily Meditation, September 23, 2016)

Meditation can help you follow *your* heart for all the answers. And it will help you discern with whom you will share your joys and struggles, and ask for guidance and opinions. People of like mind, where you hold your human truth at the same level, are of course the safest. Others will give their opinion and try to "fix" you, a topic I will cover in another chapter. The best approach is to just ask people just to hear you. Say, "I just need for you to listen and hear me here." Then just breathe and speak your truth.

Affirmation: *Divine guidance is always available to me with every breath.*

Have you ever stopped your regular meditation practice? What did you experience when stopping? Please share on my website, www.dondoninibook.com.

Affirming Until the Cows Come Home Isn't Enough

"Everyone wants to live on top of the mountain, but all the happiness and growth occur while you're climbing it." – Andy Rooney

An affirmation is positive self-talk, a statement of Truth, to bring about more good in our lives. Affirmations are important because we create our reality through our thoughts and perceptions. But you can make affirmations until the cows come home and still not reach the "top of the mountain" of your goals and desires. The important thing is that we have to "put feet" on our affirmations or do the action steps necessary to manifest them. As the late *60 Minutes* commentator Andy Rooney says, the growth and achievement happen on the way up to achieving your goal.

It is a major red flag if you are giving affirmations magical powers, so to speak, and not taking action to make a change. I was struggling financially as I started my spiritual journey when I first learned about affirmations. I thought if I affirmed hard enough that I was prosperous and abundant that God was going to go put money in my bank account. Well, of course, that didn't happen. I needed to do the action step of becoming financially *responsible* myself along with my affirmations to live abundantly. Affirmations help us quiet that monkey chatter, monkey mind, or negative thoughts from our subconscious. Affirmations help drive away the old beliefs and habits that can haunt us. Our goal is to turn up the Divine positive statements consistently, most often to drown out those old negative thoughts. Doing so brings us to a peaceful life because we can reframe each situation by affirming the good in every negative circumstance.

In her book, "You Can Heal Your Life," the metaphysical author Louis Hay says that we need to use "denials" before our affirmations to drown out these old habits and patterns causing our negative thoughts. A denial is a belief or thought that expresses our resistance to change as we deny that anything is wrong or ignore a problem that is adversely affecting our life, thinking that the issue will "just go away. One theory is that our thoughts cause our feelings and behaviors. Louise uses a garden analogy to illustrate this. Before we plant the new in our gardens, we first need to the pull the weeds in our gardens to make room for the new plants just as we have to acknowledge the old (deny) to embrace the new (affirm).

Here is an example of a denial before an affirmation: "I let go of the need to feel that people are out to get me. I am trusting." Here is another one by Louise Hay: "Any idea of age is eliminated from my mind and erased from my body. I age with grace." So you see that "denial" in this sense is not denying that you have a problem. Instead, it is denying or letting go of the negative thoughts that may have had power over you or may have been keeping you stuck in old beliefs. You can create your own denial statements starting with, "I no longer need to . . .", or "I no longer need the belief or thought . . .", or "I choose to let go of . . ." Then create a positive affirmation that will "deny" or change the negative thought.

Remember that whatever you hold in mind brings like kind, so it is important to deny the negative thought before affirming the positive. The metaphysician Charles Fillmore likens our consciousness to "a temple" and the thoughts that stand in the way of our good as "thieves and robbers." When our minds churn with thoughts that that rob our peace of mind, it is time to say "No!" or "Stop!" and affirm the Truth that all is well. Then be ready to more quickly manifest more good in your life.

Also, I hear the word love thrown around a lot, and to me it can sound trite sometimes. There's more to love than just saying, "I love you" or even affirming "I love myself." Sitting quietly one day it came to me that love is "taking action" without hurting ourselves and others. I have heard it said that faith is God in action. In Truth, God is also love, therefore taking action can be defined as love.

Are you ready to climb the mountain and embrace your journey? I have changed my life and continue to make changes in my life by "putting feet" on positive statements or affirmations. You can, too.

Affirmation: *I take the action steps I need to manifest my affirmations.*

Have you or someone in your life affirmed without demonstration? Please share on my website, www. dondoninibook.com.

Description

Spiritual Practices Cannot Cure Biological Depression

"Don't forget to take your pill, honey." – Sister Anselm, OSF

Back in the mid-1960s when one of my soulmate friends, Joanna, and I were 8th grade students in a small-town Catholic grade school, our teacher Sister Anselm gave us a fire and brimstone lecture on the evils of going to public high school. She warned us that instead of eating a nutritious lunch that we would go out back of the school for a "Coke and a smoke." (Really?) But her sternest warning revolved around our soon-to-be dating life. "Your parents will just send you out the door and say, 'Don't forget to take your pill, honey.'" At recess that day, Joanna and I tried to figure out what she was talking about. "What pill?" Joanna asked. Neither one of us had a clue that Sister Anselm was talking about the newly introduced birth control pill that was shocking the Catholic Church to its core with its implications of "free love" outside of marriage. We eventually found out what the pill was all about, but we never did choose a Coke and a smoke over a good hot lunch!

Today, I'm here to encourage you to "take your pill, honey" if you happen to be among the 15 million Americans who suffer from persistent clinical or biological depression. Yes, our spiritual practices can lead us to bliss, but watch out for the red flag of using those practices as a cure for biological ailments, especially depression. Sometimes biological depression is a roadblock to finally arriving at that blissful life we seek. In that case, we may need to see a professional for some depression medication. Yet we strongly resist that we may need an antidepressant, telling ourselves that we don't want to be dependent on a medication. Meditation should be enough, shouldn't it? That's understandable, but I have found that spiritual practices cannot cure a biological depression. That's a job for antidepressants, which can actually help to expedite your spiritual growth by tearing down the roadblock of biological depression.

Because this depression is biological, your body may already be giving you signals that your blue mood is more than simply sadness. For example, an article by Melissa Breyer, Senior Editor, *Healthy & Green Living* (http://www.care2.com/greenliving/9-physical-symptoms-of-depression.html) points out how physical pain is often an overlooked symptom of depression. Are you experiencing unexplained back pain, muscle aches, headaches, or digestive problems? Are you not sleeping well? Have you had a significant change in your weight or appetite – either increased or reduced? Check with your physician first, but be aware that these physical pains and changes are also typical signs of clinical depression that can be helped by medication and/ or psychotherapy.

I find it difficult to mentor someone who is clinically depressed because oftentimes they do not have the energy to take responsibility for their lives, which is an important step in walking and progressing on a spiritual path. I knew of someone who was struggling in her marriage, and in time I believed that clinical depression was the main factor behind her struggles and unhappy life situations. I advised her to consult with a professional for an evaluation to see if her depression had a biological cause. I had learned that one third of people who start taking antidepressants just take it as a "jump start" to help them overcome short-term challenges, while one third are on and off medication as needed, and one third choose to be on it for life. After I explained that, her response did not surprise me. She did not need antidepressants, she believed, because she practices yoga to combat her depression. Yoga is a wonderful practice for body, mind, and spirit, that is proven to complement the effects of traditional medicine and medications. However, I knew that she could practice yoga until she was blue in the face and it will not eliminate her depression if it is her *biology* that is causing it. Only antidepressants can do that.

However, a part of a spiritual journey is learning to take care of our bodies better. I know of someone who wanted so badly to drop some weight to feel and look more fit. She went from gym to gym and trainer to trainer without success, dropping out until she chose to get on a pharmaceutical for her depression. She now looks forward to going to the gym and working with her trainer at present. I praised her new, fit look when I saw her recently.

Some people also feel that taking certain herbs will alleviate a biological depression and will substitute herbs for a pharmaceutical. Many times these people will not heed the advice of a spouse or friend who advises them to seek help from a mental health professional. A clinical psychologist colleague of mine tells me that after seeing patients for 30 years he has not seen much success in treating clinical depression with herbs. He goes on to say that the most successful treatment for depression is taking a pharmaceutical accompanied by psychotherapy sessions – the overwhelming general consensus in the field of psychology. (However, I myself take herbs for promoting cardiovascular health, lower cholesterol, and healthy circulation to keep high blood pressure at bay. Ask your doctor.)

Years before, when I was studying this concept at the Unity School of Christianity, Unity Village, MO, one of my fellow students was processing what we had just learned and broke down crying in class: "I resisted for so long and I wish I would have gotten on Prozac years before." (Prozac was most often prescribed at that time.) I will always remember this. This was my wake-up call that made me look at my own resistance to seeing that I was in a biological depression years later. Antidepressant medications can expedite our spiritual growth, but it took me a while to finally accept it. I remember teaching meditation years ago, and I did a bit of "spiritual malpractice" by telling the class that with meditation they could get off their depression medicine, not realizing at the time that depression could be biological. That is what my truth was at the time. Today, I know better from experience – and now so do you.

If nothing else, take this to heart: When we have a biological depression and need to seek professional help and/or medication, it doesn't mean that we did something wrong or that we are "wrong" somehow. We are not crazy, as the old adage says. There is no shame around this. Something in the brain just isn't firing correctly. Or maybe your hormones may be out of balance. Perhaps there is a history of depression in your family. When I resisted for a year, vacillating whether or not to try an antidepressant, my therapist looked at me and said, "Do you want to be happy?" Whether your depression is biological or the result of a recent loss or unprocessed grief or other reason, a professional psychotherapist can determine the right diagnosis and the best, proven way to regain happiness and peace in your life.

The good news is that psychotherapy methods are beginning to focus on the positive aspects of a person's life as a foundation for healing the negative emotions. For example, a psychotherapist I know explained to me that some therapists are moving away from the older rational emotive theory, which posited that our thoughts create our emotions and behaviors. Referencing positive psychology, they are seeing a reversal of the starting points with someone's thoughts and actions and how they create emotional responses and actions. Now with positive psychology therapy, therapists start with positive emotions and see how they affect a person's thought-action repertoire. For example, if a person talks about all of the things going wrong in her life, the therapist might change the focus and ask her, "What are you grateful for?" Or "Where in your life do you find joy, serenity, contentment, or love?"

Also, psychotherapists are recognizing the positive aspects of meditation and other spiritual practices as an effective complement to traditional treatment. According to Gary A. Levinson, MD, Doctor of Psychiatry, *"I agree that spiritual practices cannot cure biological depression, but it can be a significant asset to psychiatric psychopharmacological treatment currently used to treat severe, especially chronic, depression."*

So, I encourage you to stay with your meditation as you progress on your spiritual path, but if you suffer from biological depression I say to you with love, "Take your pill, honey," on the advice of a professional, if needed, as you walk your spiritual path. It's really ok and it will really help.

Affirmation: *I practice healthy self-care and keep an open mind to all healing practices.*

What do you think about this chapter on depression? Please share on my website, www. dondoninibook.com.

Don't Be Afraid of the Dark

"Life is difficult." – Dr. Scott Peck

Since reading that first line of Dr. Scott Peck's *The Road Less Traveled* many years ago, I've learned firsthand that if we realize that life is difficult and choose not to run away from it, but rather face our difficulties and challenges head on and see them as opportunities, we can learn glorious things on the way to experiencing bliss in our lives. I still find this to be true as I walk my path.

As you start your spiritual journey, one of the most difficult things to do may be to sit quietly, meditate, and contemplate – and it can be surprising and scary when this practice brings up subconscious pain, regrets, and grief. Isn't meditation supposed to be a relaxing and calming experience? Of course, it can be, but it can also reveal your personal pain that St. John of the Cross called the "dark night of the soul." Avoiding this pain is a common red flag that can stall our spiritual journey. We just need to remember over and over again that God, or the Universe, gives us nothing that we can't handle. Nothing is too big for God. Richard Rohr, director of the Center for Action and Contemplation in Albuquerque, New Mexico, points out that "if we do not transform our pain, we will most assuredly transmit it."

"Grace leads us to the state of emptiness—to a momentary sense of meaninglessness—in which we ask, "What is it all for?" The spaciousness within the question allows Love to fill and enliven us." Richard Rohr, Daily Meditation, October 16, 2016.

So what happens if you do not face and transform the dark side of your pain? As Richard Rohr says, you will most likely transmit it to other areas of your life – creating drama in family and intimate relationships, prolonging traumatic situations, fueling addictive behaviors, and living in a constant state of denial, all of which makes your life even more difficult. *(Note: This is a different kind of denial that what is discussed in "Affirming Until the Cows Come Home.")*

The good news – and perhaps the bad news – is that the only way to transform your dark side and emerge on the other side is to go through it. In the Prologue to *The Ascent of Mount Carmel*, the words of John of the Cross seek to help us understand how and why we need to look deep into ourselves and not fear the dark side: *"A deeper enlightenment and wider experience than mine is necessary to explain the dark night through which a soul journeys toward that divine light of perfect union with God that is achieved, insofar as possible in this life, through love. The darknesses and trials, spiritual and temporal, that fortunate souls ordinarily undergo on their way to the high state of perfection are so numerous and profound that human science cannot understand them adequately. Nor does experience of them equip one to explain them."*

Ultimately, you have to sit with your dark side on your own. Many of us go to workshops, classes, and read all the self-help books that we can get our hands on for years. We go to different spiritual readers and mentors. These things are all helpful, but unless we take the action step to sit with our dark side we are unlikely to progress to the next plateau on our journey.

Needless to say, I have done my share of all of the above until I realized that it was really my own work to do. I realized that I already had all of the tools necessary to take the action steps to grow on my spiritual path. As my mentor told me on my final session with her, "Don, I have given you everything you need to know to progress on your journey. I am here if you need me."

As I said earlier in this book, the student now becomes the teacher. I remember mentoring someone who had been in Alcoholics Anonymous and had been sober for 22 years. However, she still appeared to be stuck in her recovery. I felt that she felt a separation from her Higher Power, so I told her that she and her Higher Power were one and cannot be separated. This is the unitive consciousness that leads us to embracing a personal God – not a God somewhere up in the sky sitting on a throne and judging us like we may have been taught in traditional religion. As we grow spiritually, we come to know a personal God who is one with us and always connected with us in a unitive consciousness. It is that Divine connection that smooths our path to spiritual growth and to recovery, if need be.

And keep in mind that things come to us in God's way and in God's time. We will know when and how to sit within darkness as we keep our prayer life going and asking Source, "What is my next best thing to do?" We must listen for the guidance and be willing to go there when the time presents itself. And we do not need to be afraid.

"You don't go through a deep personal transformation without some kind of dark night of the soul," wrote the late professor and philosopher Sam Keen. I know this truth from my own experience. I spent many, many mornings weeping as I sat quietly and my dark night of the soul presented itself. However, afterwards I felt lighter and more self-aware each time. If you choose to use a spiritual mentor or therapist, I suggest that after interviewing them, choose one and stick with them instead of running from one to another until you find one who tells you what you want to hear. The real question is, what does your soul *need* to hear? No therapist, mentor, reader, minister, rabbi, sage, or spiritual teacher can do your work for you. They can facilitate your journey, but only you can do your own work. Yes, at times it is painful and difficult, but the light of growth, peace, and bliss are waiting on the other side.

I leave you with a more lighthearted example of embracing the dark side that comes from one of my favorite "Peanuts" comic strips. Snoopy is lying on top of his doghouse trying to sleep in the pitch dark, but worrisome questions keep him awake. "Who am I? Will I come to a happy death?" haunt him in his dark night of the soul. When morning comes and the sun rises, Snoopy surrenders to sleep. Charlie Brown and his friends walk by and say, "Isn't it wonderful to be a dog? You can just sleep all the time." Snoopy opens one eye and thinks, "No, only when the sun is up." I've always thought of Snoopy's experience as the peace and light we feel on the other side after embracing our dark night of the soul.

Affirmation: *I embrace the dark night of the soul without fear on my spiritual journey.*

Have you surrendered and sat with your dark side of the soul? If so, did it bring you to a further plateau on your spiritual journey? Please share on my website, www.dondoninibook.com.

Meditation is Not an Escape from Reality

"We don't need to hide behind religious beliefs or use our relationships with our Higher Power as an excuse to stop taking responsibility for ourselves." – Melody Beattie

A student in my class when I was training for ministry was losing her house and didn't seem to have any remorse. She told me that she sits in meditation hours each day. Nothing bothered her. Yes, it does feel good to be connected to God or Source, but is not an escape from reality. Even though it is said that we live from the inside out, there is an outside called reality. We can run, but we cannot hide from our humanness and from real-world problems like losing one's home. Consider it a red flag on your spiritual path if you are using meditation to escape reality.

When it comes to wanting to stay on top of the mountain feeling peaceful instead of facing the reality of day-to-day life, I have been there, done that. When I was teaching, I would get up early and still be late for my job on a regular basis. Why? Because I could not break free from the peace and joy I felt during my morning meditation. Taking belly breaths, I would quietly work out on my weight bench. I was somewhere else with Spirit listening, and it felt so good that I procrastinated on getting ready for work. I was reprimanded by the administration so many times to the point of losing my teaching position where I was on the top of my pay scale. It took some time, but I finally learned that I could channel the peace I felt in meditation to ask for Divine guidance in how to be fully human and more responsible in the real world.

Also, Melody Beattie's words always remind me that escaping reality through meditation is simply not an option if we truly want to grow on our spiritual path: *"Our Higher Power is no substitute for relationship with people. We don't need to hide behind religious beliefs or use our relationships with our Higher Power as an excuse to stop taking responsibility for ourselves. But we can tap into and trust a Power greater than ourselves for the energy, wisdom, and guidance to do that."*

Now, I'm not saying that we need not meditate, contemplate or sit still. Try meditating a bit each day. I suggest in the morning before starting your day. As you do, just by taking a deep breath you will begin to know deep within and without yourself that you are guided by Source *every moment of every day*. Even the profound teacher Richard Rohr still finds guidance for the reality of his own life through what he calls "the prayer of quiet": *"From my own experience, I know I need a contemplative practice to rewire my mind. Some form of the prayer of quiet is necessary to touch me at the unconscious level, the level where deep and lasting transformation occurs. From my place of prayer, I am able to understand more clearly what is mine to do and have the courage to do it."*

So how can we incorporate a contemplative practice without making it an escape from reality? Just remember to breathe and stay aware of the Divine Source that is always with you. I was told that the Christian Brothers had a tradition in their schools where a daily designated prayer leader would ring a bell on the hour and say, "Let us remember that we are in the holy prescience of God". After a brief moment of silence the class would resume. Following this tradition, we could do a small thing like have our watches beep every hour or ninety minutes to remind us to take a deep, belly breath acknowledging that we are not alone in our work and play. Where we get in trouble is when we try to go it alone, but Divine help is right with us, in and through us. Call that divine help, light, universal energy, God, quantum physics, or whatever works for you. It's only a deep breath away.

Affirmation: *I am guided by God/Source every moment of every day.*

What is your name for God or Divine help? What is your method for staying connected to Spirit and reality at the same time? Please share on my website, www.dondoninibook.com.

If It's Too Good to Be True . . .

*"We don't know where our first impressions come from or precisely what they mean,
so we don't always appreciate their fragility."* – Malcolm Gladwell

I was attending a New Thought church one Sunday and sat next to a tall, dark and handsome man. After the service, we had a big hug (like I said, it was a New Thought church) and I asked him out for coffee. My motive was to pick him up, because I just knew immediately, "Sweet Jesus, my prayers have been answered!" He is metaphysical, light-hearted, like-minded and gorgeous all at the same time. I was between relationships, and my prayer at the time focused on seeking another relationship with a person with just those qualities. Go figure.

Well, I did start seeing him, and needless to say it was far from a perfect fit. I was attending church to gain more spiritual nourishment, but he was there to mainly find a relationship. In other words, I had been walking and learning on my spiritual journey for a few years already, but he was just starting on his path. As I got to know him, I found that he was attached to mostly things and corporate power. He didn't live with integrity, and he was manipulating and slick the majority of the time. He stepped on folks to get to the top of his career. I wanted him to take care of me and he wanted me to take care of him financially. (Which is neither good or bad. Taking care of each other and caretaking is different even though the semantics sound a lot alike.) Not that I was a saint either. Early on my path I had experienced some of the same issues I've mentioned about him, and that is why I could see his red flags so clearly at the time. That's called the mirror effect or, "Spot it, you got it."

The mirror effect is a concept that is often talked about in recovery programs. Once I had a boss who attended AA meetings and he would often say, "Spot it, you got it" every time I would make an assertive suggestion (or I thought constructive criticism) for him. It would infuriate me until I got it and learned more about the mirror effect. Then I began to accept more responsibility for my words and behaviors.

The "red flag" message here is: Discern or get burned. Listen to that handsome man or beautiful woman from your Christ center – really hear them and feel their energy. You will hear and feel how far the person has come on their spiritual journey. Don't assume just because you have met them with people of like mind that they are where you are on your path.

A wise spiritual teacher once wrote that most people will tell you who they really are early in a relationship, but sometimes we just can't or don't want to hear it. I learned this lesson for myself the hard way. When I had my floral design business, I had interviewed a person who said she wanted to open a business just like mine someday. Well, I did not really hear what she was saying. I hired her and trained her in floral design. I educated her in every aspect of my business with the intention of her being an asset to my success. But she had a different intention – which she had told me upfront, but I did not listen or believe her. Eventually she left her job with me to start her own floral design business and she became my competition. So I urge you to hear and believe people when they tell you who they are and what they want from you. Then discern before you allow them into your life.

I also knew of someone who, when she first started dating, met a man who told her upfront that he was a gambler. He even showed her his tax return that specified that he made a living as a gambler. She told me that she didn't want to see that red flag because she wanted to be in a relationship – not to mention that this man was very charming and good looking. She ignored his addiction and justified it by believing that gambling was not a problem. When her man starting losing at the track or at the casino, he started stealing from her to pay his debts and replenish his gambling stake. He also found other women, and men, who would feed his addiction. Eventually he ended up in prison. This woman found out the hard way that gamblers are liars. She didn't want to believe who he really was when he told her upfront.

So, even if someone is gorgeous, smart, spiritual – "perfect" for you – run like hell when you hear and feel more negative energy than positive as the relationship develops. You can still honor and love them from afar if you choose. Or if you choose to stay in their lives and get burned again in the future, discerning becomes a must if you really want to break the cycle. I had to endure several more volatile and drama-filled relationships before I learned my lesson to seriously discern. Author and healer Louise Hay writes that everyone we meet and everything we do is for a reason. So please be gentle with yourself because even when you trip up on a red flag like this, be assured that you are still on your path. As you learn to discern relationships you will find that you will learn how to love and be loved in a healthier way. At last.

Affirmation: *I discern relationships from my Christ Center.*

From a lack of discernment have you ever felt burned? Has someone told you something that was a red flag, but you pursued the relationship or situation anyway? Please share on my website, www. dondoninibook.com.

You Can Use Your New Knowledge for Good or Bad

"I am not a teacher, but an awakener." – Robert Frost

When I first started seeing my spiritual mentor, she told me that what she was going to teach me I could use for good or bad. She said that the student may one day become the teacher. As you experience spiritual growth in your own life, you can start guiding others on their spiritual journey. However, because we are already advanced on our path, farther along than others, it is easy to take advantage of others due to their undeveloped knowledge of Truth, whether we intend to or not. Also, I have found that it is important to be careful about giving the mentee too much information at one time. They may become overwhelmed or confused and miss the message you are trying to convey. Instead, offer smaller lessons so they will have time to digest the truth and apply it to their own spiritual growth.

There are two things to keep our eye on living spiritually – to avoid manipulating others and to keep our motives pure. Consider it a red flag if you notice – or someone tells you – that your words are not congruent with your behavior. Melody Beattie tells us in *The Language of Letting Go* that if someone's words do not match his or her behavior, "be ready to be controlled, manipulated, and deceived." So if you are talking the talk, but not walking the walk, you risk manipulating or deceiving others more easily – a big stumbling block on your spiritual journey.

Also, we sometimes hear the phrase "spiritual malpractice." Because we have walked our paths longer, we see a person's vulnerabilities more clearly. Also, we have developed a more spiritual self-awareness and knowledge of Truth through prayer, contemplation/meditation, working with spiritual mentors and communities, and taking action based on our knowledge. We've "got it," so when we encounter people who are just starting out on their spiritual paths we are eager to help them along – and that is where the red flag of spiritual malpractice can block their growth, and prevent us from doing the good we wish to do.

Our intentions are good, but we sometimes end up taking advantage of the people we want to help by keeping them down through manipulating, controlling, "fixing", and badgering them to embrace spiritual practices that are right for us, but not necessarily for them. Well, guess what? We may be called to mentor or teach, but we are not in charge of another's spiritual growth. God (Spirit, Inner Light, Higher Power, Source, Universal Intelligence) is the only One in charge. But we can tap into Divine guidance to help awaken others to see the growth opportunities Spirit has for them.

> *Timing is important. Only you can sense what is right for you and what will serve the highest good. Self-serving action if not applied to creating the higher good is just that. Self-serving. It isn't an easy call but generally your heart will say yes or no, and you can trust that. "Release and let go. Be what I have created you to be." Lynn Eckert, Mari & Messengers Meditation*

We are advanced on our path and we are on our own personal journey. Every person has the opportunity to do the same. There is no right or wrong way to grow spiritually if you are connected to Spirit. Also, trust that God will send you the right person — at the right time — to mentor and guide. Spiritual teacher and author Marianne Williamson writes: *"I can't imagine where I'd be today had there not been those who arrived on my path to show me what I needed to see at just the moment when I needed to see it. Now it's my turn, to try to put together some piece of life's puzzle for those who look to me as one who's done it herself."*

By the way, keep in mind that spiritual growth is a lifelong process, not a project with a deadline. That is why we refer to it as a journey, not a destination. You may have heard people say when "I get there" I will act differently or do this or that differently. I will be more blissful, peaceful, balanced, and happier. Yes, we will experience many different feelings and changes along our way, including personal human struggles and challenges to work through.

I have found through my mentoring that if I feel the pain and let go of resistance to get through these human struggles and challenges, it has brought me more positive growth, more bliss, more peace, more balance, and more happiness. Please remember there is grace for us to receive all of those good things. It gets easier if we do not resist, since we learn to live and grow spiritually from nonresistance. Blessings on your journey.

Affirmation: *I mentor others with Divine guidance from Spirit.*

Have you ever experienced spiritual malpractice, or have you tried to "fix" someone? How did that turn out? Please share on my website, www.dondoninibook.com.

What's the Payoff?

"Secondary gains are manipulative tactics to gain attention and sympathy." – Dr. James Zullo, PhD.

Always the victim. Always broke. Always sick. Always in bad relationships. Always the manipulator. Always berating others. You probably know people like this, and you probably have dealt with their anger, angst, and yes, whining, at some point in time. You may have even felt that way yourself in the past, but have moved past that stage as you've grown spiritually. So it's a red flag and a threat to your serenity if you're continually dealing with someone who is bringing you down with their angst – or if you yourself have slipped back into old negative habits. But you can get past this bump on your spiritual path by asking a deceptively simple question: What's the payoff?

I suspect that people experience a certain payoff for what they say and do when they are playing the eternal victim or manipulator. In the psychological world, that payoff is called "secondary gains" of one's actions or words. Another red flag here is holding on to these payoffs – whether our own or someone else's – and allowing them to stifle our spiritual growth.

As Dr. James Zullo notes, some people's motives are to gain attention and sympathy or pity. You know that old saying, "Bring your pity pot and let's have a pity party." And I can speak to pitiful, believe me. The payoff of my actions before my spiritual growth was that people would pity me and feel sorry for me. I was acting out of lack consciousness instead of abundance and gratitude. Why? So my dad and mom would give me money and things. So my friends would buy me drinks and dinner even though I had enough money. I was trapped in that payoff cycle until I discovered metaphysician Louis Hay and started using her affirmation, "Money comes to me in the proper time, space and sequence." As I learned to love myself and opened my mind to receive the unlimited abundance from God, of the Universe, I no longer needed the payoff of being pitied for not having enough.

I have found that when we have grown spiritually, catching our thoughts and being more conscious of them, we no longer need payoffs so emphatically. Yet, for some people the payoffs can be a way of life, and it's easy sometimes to get pulled into the drama. Maybe you know someone who is constantly feeling ill, always running from doctor to doctor, having multiple surgeries, and they allow that script to dominate their lives. Perhaps their payoff is getting attention and nurturing from their healthcare providers, as well as from family and friends. Perhaps their belief that illness brings the payoff of love and attention is the root cause of their chronic physical pain.

The secret is to be aware of our thoughts. When people tell me what awful things are happening in their lives, I ask them what have they been thinking about, or what are their thoughts. Our thoughts can create our physical illness, and conversely our physical illness can create our thoughts. I'm not discounting that physical illness exists, but I do believe that changing your thinking can lessen your pain and improve your well-being. In "You Can Heal Your Life" author Louise Hay writes: *If I had an operation to get rid of the cancer and did not clear the mental pattern that created it, then the doctors would just keep cutting Louise until there was no more Louise to cut.* So yet another red flag on your path is to be unaware of your thought processes around illness and everything that affects your life and well-being.

In another case, think of a wife who says over and over and over again how awful her husband is to her. She says things like, "I can't stand him." What does she get out of berating him? First, I feel sorry for her because she is a victim of an unloving spouse. This affects my perception of him and how I react to him whenever I meet him. This person's payoff is that she thinks I will take her side and like her better than her "awful" husband. She gets a reaction from me and anyone who will listen to her story. She's miserable, so why doesn't she seek couples counseling or get a divorce? Apparently, the payoff of getting the extra attention, approval, and pity is a greater reward than breaking free from a bad relationship.

Some people who constantly put others down, or try to control other people, are perhaps after the same payoffs. Prior to my spiritual growth, my parents enjoyed getting a *reaction* out of me. At the time I was an adult living five hours away from them, but they phoned often with the *parental* do's and don'ts. They were trying to manipulate me as they would a child, not an adult. I would start being defensive, raising my voice to where I really did not want to talk to them anymore. At the time I did keep our phone conversations very short. But as I grew spiritually, I began to not react to the parental part of the conversation when they called, letting it go in one ear and out the other. They stopped getting the payoff of getting a reaction from me, so they stopped being so parental. So when you stop giving people their expected payoff, they tend to eventually change their behavior.

Yet other people may want to manipulate others by pushing "surprise gifts" on them or constantly "helping" them as "good" friends and neighbors. Some parents may do this, too, by giving their adult children money all of the time, buying them new cars, etc. Then, these manipulators play the guilt card so you will feel obligated to do whatever they want you to do – even if you don't want to go on vacation with them, buy their granddaughter's Girl Scout cookies, go to their church revival meeting, or whatever. Their payoff is being in control – and then playing the hurt victim when you dare to say no to them after "all they've done" for you.

Sometimes these manipulative relationships become too toxic and you just have to walk away. I remember when a former love and partner called me years after our going our separate ways. He tried his best to guilt me into getting together with him. I just held out the receiver on the land line phone, laughing hysterically to myself as he did his guilt dance. I finally said to him, "I don't go there anymore." End of story. End of payoff.

Please hear me. I am not saying that people who use secondary gains or payoffs are bad or "not so good", as I like to say. We need to remember that the human part of us is vulnerable and in need of acceptance, attention, and nurturing. We all just need more love. We want to grow together in love. But playing the victim or manipulator – or giving in to the behaviors of others who play those roles – is not the way to get there.

Affirmation: *I let go of any old payoffs that stifle my spiritual growth. I am free.*

What were your payoffs that you needed to face to grow on your spiritual path? Do you still struggle with those payoffs? Please share on my website, www.dondoninibook.com.

Don't Let Anyone Pour Cold Water on Your Dreams

"As I say yes to life, life says yes to me." – Louise Hay

At 45 years old I was first introduced to self-care as I experienced massage, reiki (energy work), and spiritual mentoring while attending a 12 Step program. My dream to pursue my life's work in self-care, body work, and healing all started after I listened to an audio series by Jack Canfield, *Self Esteem and Peak Performance*. But the path to realizing that dream was paved with far many more red flags than I ever expected.

At that time I had a fairly successful business of 15 years planning weddings, parties and meetings where we specialized in florals and props. Truthfully, I was burnt out doing my business and not worthy to charge what I was worth for my skills. I was paying everyone else and leaving little for me. My big ego -- getting praise and recognition from my customers for making things pretty -- was my emotional pay off. But it certainly didn't make me rich or pay the bills, even after 15 years of working 16 hours a day.

What I really wanted was to be a massage therapist, a reiki practitioner, and a spiritual mentor – not uncommon after diligently working a spiritual path. After experiencing the wonder of self-care through body work, I wanted to be a healer. It was also the height of the AIDS crisis at the time, and I wanted to make a difference and work with this population and bring healing care to them. But too many significant people in my life discouraged me from leaving my wedding planning business. My spiritual mentor, my massage therapist, and my dad all kept pouring cold water on my dreams.

Roadblocks seemed to pop up everywhere I went. My dad kept telling me to just go back to teaching so "you can have more retirement income." My therapist said to me, "Healers are a dime a dozen." She told me not to leave my business, because she said I was so good at planning and executing wedding and parties, and after all, I had a successful business. Well, it looked successful from the outside, anyway. It reminded me of the old saying, "You are good at eating poop so continue to eat poop." But I felt so strongly about my dream that I somehow shook off the naysayers. Finally, I said "yes" to my dreams, my life, and they said "yes" to me.

I left my business and pursued the healing arts which I have been doing for 15 years and, I should add, successfully. I have learned that I am worthy to be highly compensated for my healing skills and spiritual direction, despite the popular notion that spiritual mentoring, like church, should be free since it comes from Spirit. But we are all human with bills to pay and other financial obligations. So never sell yourself short when valuing your services in the healing arts.

So the red flag here is to watch out for the naysayers. Never let others pour cold water on your dreams. Why are they doing that, anyway? Because they are jealous? Afraid to take a risk themselves? Afraid of failing or being successful? Lack of trusting themselves or taking calculated risks? You may never know their motives, and that's ok. The important thing to know is that you can overcome this common obstacle on your spiritual path.

Are you allowing other people to discourage you from achieving your dreams? Here's some inspiration for getting around this red flag. In the movie "Joy" actress Jennifer Lawrence plays Joy Mangano, a young housewife whose dreams of patenting her own inventions were continually squelched by so-called "well meaning" family members. But despite a constant barraging of negative comments – "You just can't do it, Joy. It will never work, Joy. You were wrong, Joy." – and unscrupulous business partners, Joy persevered to invent and patent the first detachable, self-wringing mop and sell it herself on the QVC Shopping Network. Today, the woman who was told "You can't" and who nearly went bankrupt in the early 1990s has her own company, holds more than 100 patents, and has an estimated net worth of approximately $50 million. Watch the movie and learn how one creative woman did not allow anyone to pour cold water on her dreams!

But look what can happen when someone is literally loved into successfully achieving a dream. Jazz legend Duke Ellington was asked by an interviewer to describe the struggles he faced in the early days of forming a band and pursuing his music. Ellington replied that he had not been a typical starving, suffering musician. "I started out doing what I most liked to do, working with music," Ellington said. "I had faith in myself and it was easy because I was so loved as a little boy. I was loved so much and held so much. I don't think my feet hit the ground until I was seven years old." See how powerful unconditional and affirming love can be!

In her messages, inspirational speaker and author Esther Hicks has said that we never lose our dreams and that they are just put on the back burner waiting for us to access them. I say fire up the stove and start cooking. Be inspired by Joy and other people like the successful crime novel author Linda Fairstein who finally embraced her lifelong dream of writing books after a 20-plus-year career as a New York crime attorney. Don't let your dreams become spoiled by negative people who constantly discourage you. Like Louise Hay, say "yes" to life and your dreams.

Affirmation: *I am worthy and highly compensated for my talent and skills.*

Do you have people in your life like Joy or like Duke? Please share on my website, www. dondoninibookcom.

Feeling Lonely or Just Alone? Yes, There's a Difference

"I once heard that the reason we need to be alone is to find out that we are never alone. God is always with us in body, mind, spirit, soul, and heart unless we disconnect and go it alone." – August Gold

It takes being alone – self-imposed times of quiet and contemplation – to start and progress on our spiritual paths, and at times it feels very lonely. When I started walking my path years ago, a spiritual way of living was not as trendy as it is today. Matter of fact, when I needed to choose a spiritual path there was only one mainstream metaphysical bookstore in the entire Chicago area at a New Thought church. No wonder I felt so lonely! And I know lonely, growing up in my generation in a small southern Illinois town to Italian Roman Catholic parents as a boy who felt different.

But I learned that there is a difference between aloneness and loneliness. In previous chapters of this book, you've learned that you need to slow down, sit still, and be quiet to grow on your spiritual journey. I love what the vibrant Unity minister Patty Pipia once wrote in her "Tidbits from Spirit" blog: "'Be still and know that I am God.' A modern day version of this is, 'Sit down, shut up, and just listen for the stillness to speak.'"

This alone time is your opportunity to do your work, embracing your dark side of night. As you sit still whatever comes up, I promise it will not eat you up because Spirit does not give us anything that we cannot handle. It may feel like it, but rest assured it will not. Nothing is bigger than God and His/Her grace and mercy.

But we are human and this alone time often makes us feel lonely. We become afraid of that loneliness and sometimes we run to people and relationships just to fill the void. I have seen people stay in terrible, unhealthy, abusive relationships for the fear of being alone. I do get it, and I have done it more than once. Running from our aloneness masked as loneliness is a huge obstacle that can derail you from your spiritual path. So trust God and trust yourself to embrace your aloneness when you are ready.

Not to say that it's an easy journey. I had moved my business from a storefront with a large apartment overlooking a lake to a storefront with only two rooms for my living quarters. I remember feeling so alone when awaking in the morning that I cried many, many days as I was studying my spiritual principles and before I found people of like mind in New Thought churches and recovery programs. Keep the faith that there are people of like mind to share and care with. Your journey will get easier!

> *"I like the idea of isolation. I like the idea of solitude. You can be connected and have a phone and still be lonely."* Paul Theroux

But along the way I was sidetracked by running away from myself and my aloneness by filling every moment of my day with other people and obligations. My clairvoyant spiritual mentor emphatically told me, "Don, you have to start saying no to people. You can't be everything to everybody. You are running in circles chasing your tail!" She was right. I really was chasing my tail working two extra jobs besides my full time teaching position where I made a good living. This is when she mentioned and introduced me to meditation to slow me down to be ok with being alone. It was painful at times, especially at first. It was then I came to know that the meditation was part of my journey to a workable life for myself. Since then I haven't stopped mediating, contemplating, through good times and not such good times. And it seems my not so good times usually happen when I cut back on my meditation and quiet time. See the connection there?

Remember, as you walk your spiritual path people will either embrace the light that you have developed or run from it. When they run, it is your opportunity to embrace your alone time and learn to be with and enjoy yourself when others are not – or choose not to be – available for you. I knew of someone whose long-term relationship had ended and he felt very lonely. I told him that in that alone time he could learn to be with and enjoy his own company. We've all heard the expression, "If you can't be with yourself, how can you have a successful relationship with someone else?" It's important that we learn to be alone with ourselves before we learn how to be in relationship with a significant other or life partner. In my father's generation, men in particular rarely experienced living alone or being with themselves. They went from their mothers taking care of them, to their wives taking care of them, to either the priesthood or the military taking care of them. That is why, as I see it, that relationships and marriages ended. Also, women were not encouraged to leave their parents' home until they got married, a practice still prevalent in some cultures.

So, if you find yourself living alone for the first time in your life, let go of the fear of getting to know yourself. Take yourself out for a movie or dinner. Be open to the experience and treat yourself like a treasured friend or partner.

That's not to say you can't reach out to like-minded people when you need encouragement and help along your journey. Some people may choose to go into recovery for an addiction. For some people, this could be their opportunity to choose to sit quietly, embrace the dark side, and then come out on the other side of it to a more blissful life. They rely on their 12 Step friends and others of like mind to help them get through it.

But sometimes even that is not enough to heal what Unity minister Ed Kosak calls the "sacred ache" that only our connectedness to your personal God can take away. I leave you with Rev. Kosak's divinely inspired words. Blessings on your journey.

"Sacred Ache"
Sometimes we need a God with skin. And sometimes . . .
When there is a deep loneliness,
When there's a terrible ache that simply cannot be assuaged by any person or thing or drug or food,
when there is longing as deep as the sea,
when there are unhealthy urges so strong,
when there is an emptiness that knows no bottom:
when there is a feeling of I am no good;
when life lacks purpose.

It is at times like these that I quit blaming everyone for these experiences. And that sacred ache leads me to my oneness with you My God, my Lord, my Christ, my Yahweh, sweet spirit, Allah, great creator, Unified field, pure potentiality, to the source, Krishna consciousness, pure consciousness, source and substance, pure intelligence, underpinning of everything that is, that which keeps the universe together. This puts a balm on that deep ache and fills up that deep longing. I look to the experience of you to soothe the Sacred Ache. I look to the experience of you to complete me, though in truth I am you. You are the life of my life, the breath of my breath, the heart of my heart, flesh of my flesh, bone of my bone.

You are in every cell muscle fiber feeling and thought. You ARE every muscle cell fiber feeling and thought of my being.

You are me, I am you. The Sacred Ache IS you. It is as if the ache is you calling out for me. And when I feel my oneness with you, the pain, the ache, is diminished. And I am grateful.
-- Rev. Ed Kosak

Affirmation: *I choose the richness of myself in contemplation.*

Have you ever lived alone? Can you be with yourself? Please share on my website, www. dondoninibook.com.

I Thought I Was Done With This

"I once was told that spiritual growth is like a spiral – painful, ugly things reappear but dissipate more quickly." – Don Donini

Think of a spiritual tool box, and as we grow spiritually we add to our tool boxes. We learn to slow down, sit quietly in meditation, use affirmations or positive statements, breathe from our bellies, live Truth, take responsibility for our own lives, trust ourselves and others, have clean motives, stop being a victim, and embrace other positive practices.

But at times the issues we thought we've already worked through reappear. I remember being disappointed and upset with myself when things I worked through began to come up again and again in my life. It had me doubting all of the self-awareness work I had diligently, painfully got past. Darn, God, I thought, I did my work, embraced my dark side of night and got past these unhealthy, negative issues, but I am again feeling jealous, unforgiving, judgmental, doubting, distrusting, feeling sorry for myself, and fearful. I often refer to these things as a dark cloud looming over me or carrying around a big log on my shoulders.

Another issue that tends to reappear is wanting to fix people before they ask me to. I have gotten together with a new friend recently and each time in her conversation she keeps beating herself up about the past and present. She keeps talking about the things she needs to do to simplify her life, but never seems to do them. Well, she is perfect prey for me, the fixer. She may have run away from me after I told her what to do and how to heal her life (telling her to order the book "How to Heal Your Life" by Louis Hay). She did not ask for me to help her change, nor did she come back to me for mentoring.(She must be happy with her miserable self as "I" see it.) What a lesson that was for me on setting boundaries! If you meet someone or have a friend whom you think needs help, hand them your business card and tell them that you do mentoring for the human spirit. Then ask them to make an appointment. And be financially compensated for the work. I have given my time away sometimes, and then I start resenting it. I start to feel that the people I mentor are taking advantage of me, but it is because I did not set boundaries with them from the get go.

I thought I was done with this dark cloud of negativity and the obsession to fix people, but I see now that it is a red flag to think that way. Life is an ebb and flow of positive and negative experiences and emotions, and in our humanness we feel it all. Honoring your feelings is important. But walking a spiritual path can give us the right insights and balance to keep us moving forward as we navigate our lives.

So now when old issues flare up and I feel the heavy, dark looming cloud, in my quiet time I ask God to please tell me what I need to know, what thoughts I need to change, what I need to learn so this heaviness I am feeling goes away. And as I listen and listen and listen and act on the guidance, things dissipate to *peacefulness* once again. Sometimes that guidance and peace have come to me in the form of spiritual writings, such as the "Advent 2016" Unity publication: "As we are constantly ourselves anew, there will always be fear, old beliefs, perhaps even relationships that resist the Light. They may be very familiar, very comfortable: but they need to be loving released through a personal relationship with Spirit, God."

> *"We are never starting over [on our spiritual journey]. In recovery [from co-dependence] we are moving forward in a perfectly planned progression of lessons. . . No, the lessons are not painful. We will arrive at that place where we can learn, not from pain, but from joy and love."*
> Melody Beattie, *The Language of Letting Go*

I was taught that when negative issues or thoughts surface again that it is like a spiral. The negative things that we have done our work around *spiral* up. So I thought well, don't fret. Just open your spiritual tool box and use the tools you have learned and collected along your journey. They have worked for you in the past, and they will work again. And they seem to work faster and faster to dissipate the negative issues as you continue to grow spiritually. Remember – you are so wise! You have the tools at hand and you know how to use them. Blessings on your journey.

Affirmation: *"I have all of the tools to overcome any roadblocks on my spiritual journey."*

Have you struggled with old issues that resurface? What spiritual tools do you use to get back on your spiritual path? Please share on my website, www.dondoninibook.com.

Live Your Truth, But Don't Proselytize

"The Twelfth Step says that having a spiritual wakening, we try to carry this message to others. How do we carry it? Not by rescuing. Not by controlling. Not by obsessing. Not by becoming evangelists for the cause." – Melody Beattie

Proselytizing used to have a benign definition of "missionary activity" or evangelizing, but today it has taken on a more negative meaning – namely, an overzealous "in your face" approach to converting people to your way of thinking and spiritual truth. Guess what, folks. It doesn't work. The need to proselytize or trying to force your new-found spiritual truths on others is a common red flag on one's spiritual journey. But you can overcome it if you just let go, let God, and let your actions inspire others to seek their own path.

Listening to a "Pray-as-You-Go" podcast (10/18/17) gave me some insight on this. When you begin to see yourself as a believer in Truth, it is easy to think that your job is to bring God to people. However, keep in mind that everywhere you go, whoever you encounter, God has been there first. God is already present and working in the lives of everyone, so your job is more to show by example how God is working in your own life rather than preaching or proselytizing.

As a kid, I always ran away from my Baptist friends who were proselytizing. Of course, what I had learned early on was that my church was the only true church established by God. I will let you guess which religion that is. Now I know there are many paths (faiths, religions, teachings) to the same God. But early in my spiritual journey as I became more self-aware, I wanted to tell the world about my new-found truth and get everyone I knew on board so they could experience more bliss, too. But I unknowingly started proselytizing much like my childhood Baptist friends, and it had the opposite effect. Instead of inspiring people to walk a spiritual path, I was turning them off.

I was hired to be a freelance commentator at floral design shows where I would do hands-on design presentations on stage. After working with my spiritual mentor and growing spiritually for a while, I started adding small spiritual insights to my presentations on stage that didn't relate to the floral designs. Not realizing

I was proselytizing, soon I was not asked back by the companies that had hired me to do the shows. I really was just being my new found self, I thought, but I realized later that pushing a spiritual message was one of the major reasons that I wasn't invited back. The people at these companies could no longer "get me" or understand who I had become as I shared the insights that my spiritual mentor had taught me. But later I understood that what I was doing was inappropriate for the situation.

Also, my staff at my own business thought I was going crazy as I started playing meditation CDs, Louis Hay affirmations, and other New Thought messages over the sound system at work. I was excited about what I had been learning and wanted to share it with my staff. But this new way of thinking was so not on their radar that they thought I was losing it. Again, I was proselytizing with good intentions, but the good was not coming through.

Overall, as I was spiritually growing I felt more peace and more balance, and I wanted to stand on my soap box and share it with everyone. Not a good Idea. It is a definite red flag if you find yourself doing this. Sharing your truth in times or places where it is inappropriate can be a huge obstacle to your spiritual growth and sometimes the growth of the very persons you want to help. But there are people you can share it with – those of like mind. Yet sometimes we just want to shake those people who are struggling, living hell here on earth, always in drama and causing trauma. We want to help people who are struggling because they have not yet learned to embrace their Divine selves. We want to tell them that they do not have to do it alone – that there is this guiding force in the universe, a good *personal* God. But before you tell them and risk proselytizing, just show them your truth in how you live your life. As Richard Rohr writes, "In the beginning, you tend to think that God really cares about your exact posture, the exact day of the week for public prayer, the authorship and wording of your prayers, and other such things. Once your life has become a constant communion, you know that all the techniques, formulas, sacraments, and practices were just a dress rehearsal for the real thing – life itself – which can actually become a constant intentional and loving prayer."

Proselytizing isn't the answer. We don't have to toot our truth like a loud foghorn. All we have to do is just live it, model it, and the people who want it will come forth to ask us to lead them in their own self-discovery adventure. And we can continue to grow on our own wonderful spiritual path knowing that we showed others the way.

Affirmation: *I live my spiritual truth now. I am truth.*

Has someone in your life made a difference in your spiritual growth by just living and modeling their truth? Please share on my website, www.dondoninibook.com.

Be Honest and Vulnerable, But Don't Expect It From Everyone

"You're only as sick as your secrets." – The Twelve Steps of Alcoholics Anonymous

As I grew, I became more open to sharing who I am and how I had grown spiritually. I thought people would be more open to share who they are, too. Not necessarily, I have found. I am loud about who I am and I am proud of the person I have become. I am an open book. But is that good or not so good?

Step 5 in Twelve Step programs offers these words for recovery: "You're only as sick as your secrets." In other words, being honest and transparent with yourself about your struggles and desires – and what you will or will not do in a relationship – is a vital part of the healing process. This honesty works the same way to further us along our path of spiritual growth. Chicago psychologist Dr. James Zullo, Ph.D., instills in people that it is vital to have an intimate person (as well as a personal God) with whom to share our stories. Keeping it all inside -- hiding fears, desires, and struggles – can trigger addiction, depression, and even physical illness. Remember that these dis-eases can block you from progressing along your spiritual path, but living and speaking your truth will knock down those barriers.

As I became more rigorously honest through my spiritual work, I felt that people would reciprocate and be honest with me. I learned, however, that we may not get honesty back from some people, and I learned to tell if someone is being dishonest. You learn not to trust these people who fabricate the truth mainly because they do not trust themselves. In my commitment to honesty and transparency of character, I became a "person of my word." When I say I will do something, I follow through on it instead of just telling people the "yes" they want to hear. I expected that other people would do the same, but you can't count on that from everyone. I know someone who talks and talks but rarely does what they are saying they are going to do. I choose not to associate with this person, and when I need to I let it go in one ear and out the other. That's how I take care of myself in those situations.

How can you be a "person of your word" and take care of yourself at the same time? First, watch out for using definitive words like "I will" or "for sure" when people are asking you to do something. Stop, take a breath, and think before you respond "yes" instantly. Make sure in your own mind and heart that you really want to do what is being asked of you. So instead of saying, "I will meet you" or "I will loan you the money," you can say "I may meet you" or "I'll plan to meet you." You can say, "Let me think about giving you a loan," or "Let me sleep on it and I will get back to you." I'm not saying not to make commitments to people or activities you want to do, but when you do say "I will," be sure to follow through and be a person of your word.

I suggest to my mentees that if you really do not want to be somewhere or with someone, whether friends or family, put a date with yourself on your calendar – maybe a pizza and a movie with your name – and then tell them that you already have a commitment. Put it on your calendar before you decline the other invitation, though, to keep with the principle of honesty – with yourself and others. The result is that you will spend your time with the people who enhance your life, as this quote from John Lennon reminds us: "Being honest may not get you a lot of friends, but it will get you the right ones instead."

So why are some of us so secretive and reluctant to speak our truth when the truth sets us free? Why are so many of us not willing to share? Fear. But why are we so afraid for people to know who we really are? Why can't we share more of our secrets? Why so afraid to "come out of the closet" so to speak? Why do we choose to be imprisoned in our closets instead of coming out, sharing our foibles (everyone has them), our sexual identity, our recovery, money issues?

I suppose the reason why some of us are not transparent in return is that we are afraid to be judged by others. We fear that others will be jealous of us and use it against us. Fear breeds more fear.

As it is said, whatever we fear (the majority of the time) will come true. It is how we were conditioned. But we can change. As we grow into our Divine selves and become fearless, and choose to trust in the universe, in the Divine, you will find it is very difficult to be with someone who is overly fearful and constantly obsessive about it. When I am around someone who is fearful, I can feel my heart closing and my stomach tightening probably because once *I was there* and I now know the freedom on the other side of the fear.

The good news is that as we grow spiritually, we no longer fear as readily. We become rather fearless. But sadly, there will still be people who will judge us and be jealous of us and use it for their own good. These are the people whom we need to discard from our lives. Let them go ASAP. Remember: People can only hurt our humanness, which is real. They cannot hurt the Divine part of us. So as we grow bigger in Spirit we can acknowledge the hurt, put a light around it, and let it go more easily. As Richard Rohr so beautifully explains:

"As you spiritually mature, you can forgive your own—and others'—mistakes. You can let go of everyone who hurt you, your former spouse, the boss who fired you, the church, or even God. You have no interest in carrying around negative baggage. Wisdom emerges when you can see everything, you eliminate none of it, and you include all as important training. Finally, everything belongs. You are eventually able to say, from some larger place that may surprise you, "It is what it is" and "Even the 'bad' was good." Richard Rohr Meditation, January 31, 2017: "See Everything; Judge Little; Forgive Much"

To paraphrase from "I Ain't Much, Baby – But I'm All I've Got" by Jess Lair, being real brings love into our lives. He defines love as sharing from the deepest part of your heart – your joys, mistakes, foibles – and getting it all back from the deepest part of the heart of another person. That's how you will find people who will embrace your transparency and vulnerability, and will reciprocate. They become your new family. These are the people of "like mind" – kindred spirits – who are growing spiritually through a recovery program, a New Thought Church or Spiritual Center, traditional congregations, group therapy, mentoring groups, and other areas of your life. Social media can be another avenue in which many people choose to express their vulnerability and disclose the intimate details of their lives. In all cases, first sit quietly and discern carefully in your heart center before sharing your intimate stories with anyone. Remember, the truth will set you free. Blessings on your journey.

Affirmation: *I am a person of my word.*

Were you ever frustrated sharing from your deepest heart and not getting it back? Please share on my website, www.dondoninibook.com.

Don't Isolate Yourself on the Mountain

"Solitude vivifies; isolation kills." – Joseph Roux

As we grow spiritually, we are more energetically aware because we feel energy more readily. It can affect our mood and even our entire being. We feel the energy of others, good or not so good. We know what good energy feels like, such as when you are in the company of like-minded, positive, encouraging people. We've been to the mountain of peace and positive energy and we love it there. But as you grow, you will also pick up the bad vibes of energy vampires – the people and situations that suck the energy right out of you. If you've ever spent time around certain people at work or play and afterwards felt emotionally and energetically drained and negative, then you have experienced energy vampires.

So it's no surprise that the more we meditate – feel that connection and peace – and grow spiritually we may want to just hibernate or isolate ourselves in safe places, like our homes, where we are not affected by others' negative energies. For example, my spiritual mentor did not hibernate at home, but she would always keep her bedroom door shut when she had social gatherings at her house to keep the energy clean in that room. We can take similar actions to keep our own personal spaces clean and free of negative energy.

We want to stay on top of the mountain in the good positive light and feel the good energy that we've created for ourselves. But it's a big red flag if you begin to isolate yourself from other people just to avoid coming in contact with negative energy. Staying on top of the mountain can be dangerous to our spiritual and even physical health alike. Without socializing face-to-face with people on a regular basis, we age more quickly, and research has proven it. AARP published a list of ten things that keep people younger, and at the top of that list is personally socializing with others. Also, the research of Robert Waldinger, M.D., the director of the Harvard Study of Adult Development and a Zen priest, indicates that building strong personal relationships with people can positively influence the quality of our health as we age. Loneliness or isolation from other people, Waldinger found, is just as harmful to one's health as smoking and alcoholism.

Well, you may say, I socialize every day with hundreds of people on Facebook, Twitter, and other social media sites. But even if you "see" the "friends" on these sites through photos and written posts, you are still missing out on the live, face-to-face energy that keeps us engaged and alive. Social media, while it has its place, unfortunately makes it easier to isolate oneself and more difficult to feel the emotions of in-person relationships.

The good news is that you can still be around people of all kinds of different energies, good and bad, without absorbing the negative energies and making them your own. I learned, and now teach, some techniques to help you avoid taking in negative energy, especially when you are in the presence of people of unlike mind. (However, I do suggest that you try to spend less and less time with people of unlike mind, even if they are family.)

One technique is to visualize white light around you, like the sunlight shining on a lake or the ocean. Visualize it starting at the top of your head and moving down, covering your entire body. A second technique is to visualize standing in a ring of fire. The third is to see yourself covered in mirrors so that people's negative energies and projections reflect back to them.

Also, I suggest limiting time with people who project negative energy if we absolutely must be around them, such as at work. Think of them as ten-minute people, five-minute people, and even one-minute people. A one-minute person is the one you pass while entering work, say hello, good day, and then scamper away. As you are spiritually growing, your parents, brothers, and sisters who create negative energy may be five or ten-minute people. After a five or ten-minute phone call, for example, you can just say, "Got to go. Talk to you later," without justifying or offering a reason why.

So you don't need to isolate yourself from people and situations with negative energy, because you'll only be hurting yourself. Catholic parish priest, poet, and philosopher Joseph Roux goes as far to say that "isolation kills" – body, mind, and spirit – while the solitude that goes hand in hand with meditation and contemplation "vivifies" or energizes one's life.

Along with making you age faster, isolation can exacerbate an addiction, especially if you already have an addictive personality. It could also heighten depression because you are disconnected from personal contact. Most of all, isolation is such a red flag because it can also cause you to shut down your vulnerable and transparent side, causing you to become emotionally constipated – and keep you from growing in self-awareness and one with Spirit. Remember that quiet time alone on the mountain of meditation is going to get you further along your spiritual path, but isolation can be a major roadblock. Yes, there is negative energy out there, but you don't have to hide from it.

Affirmation: *I choose the positive energy of solitude in contemplation.*

Is isolating who you have become? If so, do you recommend others do the same? Please share on my website, www.dondoninibook.com.

Never Forget How Far You Have Come on Your Journey

"Remind yourself that you cannot fail at being yourself." – Dr. Wayne W. Dyer

Another typical red flag to watch out for is becoming discouraged and beating ourselves up for not growing faster on our spiritual journey – for not seeing things more readily that tend to derail us even if for a short time. You wonder: Why am I not more intuitive? Why do I still feel stuck? Why do I still experience "stinking thinking"?

What's really happening here is what I call spiritual amnesia. You've forgotten how far you have already come on your spiritual journey. Your mind dwells on the negative and that old feeling that you just aren't good enough or smart enough or spiritual enough to be farther along. It's time to throw that red flag away.

Instead dwell on how far you have come, because you have many positive successes if you have been on your journey awhile. Sit quietly and pray and think about where you were when you started walking your spiritual path. Keep a notebook and a pen handy and jot down words that come to you to elaborate on later. Are you less critical, less judging, less resentful, less blaming? Are you happier, and more responsible for yourself and behaviors? Are you less angry? How have you changed and how has it changed your approach to life? If you have been journaling from the beginning, get out your notebook and review what you have written over time. Your words will reveal your growth. If you happen to see where you need more improvement, please be gentle with yourself. You have come a long way. Also, listen to people as they praise you on your growth and receive the gift of positive energy they send your way.

I recall a couple of ways that I could see how much I had grown spiritually. Whenever I went to visit family I would go to Catholic Mass with my parents. After Mass on the way home, my mom and dad would judge and criticize friends who had been at that Sunday's service. One time I became very quiet (those who know me know that is unusual for me). At that point my mom said to me, "Donald, you don't criticize people anymore." I thought wow, they see my growth, and most importantly I recognized my own growth.

Recognizing your growth can have a life changing impact on your life, as Oprah Winfrey writes: "When you surrender and stop resisting and stop trying to change that which you can't change, but be in the moment, be fully open to the blessings you've already received and those that are yet come and stand in the space of gratitude . . . and look at where you are and how far you've come and what you've accomplished – when you can claim THAT and SEE that, the literal vibration of your life will change."

As I mentioned throughout the book, spiritual growth is a process. I need to constantly be aware of my words so as not to judge and criticize others and myself, since I was steeped in it when growing up in our home. Now when I want to judge, I just have to say to myself emphatically: STOP! I also now stop myself from judging by repeating to myself, "The Christ" – the spiritual part of self within everyone. In the past if I saw someone obese, or very thin, or unkempt, or a different race or culture, someone transitional in gender, or someone introverted (since I am extroverted off the scale), I would start to judge. Today I repeat over and over "The Christ" until that criticizing energy disappears. Pick a centering word or phrase that works for you.

I honor and respect your growth and any foibles you have along the way. Keep on keeping on. Blessings on your journey.

Affirmation: *I am grateful for my growth.*

Are you focusing on how far you have come or are you beating yourself up about not growing as fast as you think you should have? Please share on my website, www.dondoninibook.com.

No Turning Back

"Teachers open the door. You enter by yourself." – Chinese Proverb

"This is your last chance. After this, there is no turning back. You take the blue pill - the story ends, you wake up in your bed and believe whatever you want to believe. You take the red pill - you stay in Wonderland and I show you how deep the rabbit-hole goes." Morpheus in "The Matrix"

I remember meeting with my spiritual mentor and telling her in an angry tone after working with her for a year, "I want to turn back. I don't want to do this spiritual stuff, journey anymore." She took a drag from her cigarette and heard me out. Her response was, "It wasn't any better before, was it?" Hello!

Walking a spiritual path forces us to make a decision whether to stay blissfully ignorant and stuck in our old familiar ways that really do not work for us – but we stay there because we think it's too much work or too painful to grow past them – or to face the reality and truth of our situation and be willing to do whatever it takes to grow spiritually. The movie "The Matrix" offers what I see as a good example of this spiritual challenge.

In the film, the main character, Neo, is offered the choice between a red pill and a blue pill. The blue pill represents falsehood, security and the blissful ignorance of illusion that exists in the Matrix. The red pill imparts knowledge, freedom and the sometimes the painful truth of reality – and would allow Neo to escape from the Matrix and enter the real world. But life would be harsher and more difficult than in the Matrix where Neo lived in a simulated and comfortable world in a cocoon of false security. In the Matrix, Neo lives as a programmed "loyal soldier" who goes along with the rules of the teachings he was programmed to believe and follow – and never to question. But if he takes the red pill, he would be forced to question and possibly reject everything we was taught to believe. He would no longer have the fantasy world of the Matrix to protect him, but he would finally become free to find real, personal meaning to his life, just as we do when we embrace our own personal spiritual adventure.

Richard Rohr writes of the "loyal soldier" in his book, *Falling Upward*, which discusses how dying to our false self – the self who blindly follows the rules out of guilt, shame, or fear – is the only way to discharge our inner loyal soldier and become who we were meant to be in God. Rohr states: "The Loyal Soldier wears the common disguise of loyalty, obedience, and old-time religion, which is all you have until you have experienced undeserved and unmerited love. In order to move to the second half of life, we must respect, honor, and create closure for our Loyal Soldier. We need to "discharge" the Loyal Soldier because he or she has been in charge most of our lives. This stalwart part of our psyche has tried to protect us, but the time comes to let it rest so that we can live more authentically in peace and freedom."

When we choose and take the red pill of the reality of spiritual growth, it is difficult to turn back because we have grown past the old which no longer works as readily for us anymore. What makes us want to go back to the old is that our new way of living is too vague and not clear to us yet. This limbo of time between quitting our old habits and beginning our new spiritual path is called different things – being in the wilderness or in the land of uncertainty. Unity calls this period chemicalization. It feels strange and uncomfortable. Emile Cady in her book, "Lesson in Truth," explains it this way: "There has been a clash between the old condition – which was based on falsehood, fear and wrong ways of thinking – and the new thought of Truth entering into you."

Needless to say that I finally got it, hung in there, and have walked my spiritual journey ever since. But do I at times doubt, get frustrated, and want to quit my walk? Do I sometimes think I've taken the wrong colored pill? Yes, but the fibers and cells of my being tell me to persevere and keep on walking even though I have had to walk away from people who profess the old in my life. The great thing is as a walk I feel new fellow seekers walking beside me, encouraging me. I just need to keep reminding myself that the grass wasn't greener on the other side and how it wasn't any better before. I really do not want to return to the matrix of the more dysfunctional life I had before I started walking on my spiritual path. As you grow and travel further along your own spiritual path, you, too will find kindred spirits in your life who will encourage you to not look back, but rather keep moving forward toward your personal spiritual Truth.

And now, as this journey we have shared together in this book comes to a close, I will leave you with this reading from Unity's *Daily Word* to encourage you to celebrate yourself as your true self unfolds along your spiritual path:

"I am an active participant in life's unfolding. Even the smallest moments are worthy of celebration because I am reflecting God in all that I think, say, and do. As I express reverence and appreciation for what might seem like minor triumphs, I empower more of what I want, rather than what I do not want. I celebrate my spiritual growth, rejoicing in the times I took the high road in conflict, the moments I chose love over a compulsion to be seen as right. Perhaps I choose to applaud the time I asked for needed help—and actually received it. Or I might elect to honor the moment I mustered the courage to speak my truth. I recognize and celebrate my accomplishments and my spiritual growth."

Affirmation: *I recognize and celebrate my spiritual growth.*

What is your experience on your spiritual journey? Have you ever wanted to turn back? How did you work through that challenge? Please share on my website, www.dondoninibook.com.

Appendix

Suggested Reading List

Melody Beattie, *The Language of Letting Go*

Dr. Wayne Dwyer, *The Power of Intention*

Edwene Gaines, *The Four Spiritual Laws of Prosperity*

Louise Hay, *You Can Heal Your Life*

Vernon Howard, *The Power to Say No*

Jess Lair, *I Ain't Much, Baby – But I'm All I've Got*

Mother Teresa, *A Simple Path*

Mary Oliver, "The Summer's Day" (poem)

M. Scott Peck, M.D., *The Road Less Traveled*

John Powell, SJ, *Happiness is an Inside Job*

Fr. Richard Rohr, OSF, *Falling Upward*

John "Jack" Shea, *An Experience of Spirit: Spirituality and Storytelling*

Printed in the United States
By Bookmasters